TALES OF FISHING

BRYN HAMMOND

The
Halcyon
Press

Published by

The Halcyon Press.

A division of

Halcyon Publishing Ltd.

P.O. Box 360, Auckland, New Zealand.

Printed through
Bookprint International Limited
Hong Kong

ISBN 1-877256-09-9
Copyright Bryn Hammond © 2001
First Published 2001
All Rights Reserved

Illustrations from original watercolours by Nancy Tichborne
© Nancy Tichborne
From: *Anglers Paradise* by Nancy Tichborne and Bryan Tichborne
Published by The Bush Press, 1990

CONTENTS

Philosophers and other wise men tell us it is not possible to step into the same river twice; a concept many fly-fishermen understand evenmoreso than most philosophical men.

The following tales of fishing are perhaps about attempts to step into the same rivers again and again, penetrating the unchanging shimmering veil of water.

INTRODUCTION

The tales of fishing and other peripheral delights recounted in this book are not set out in any chronological order. Some of the tales they tell happened in hours or days snatched away from ships in which I sailed.

Not all ports of call afforded me the chance of fishing, although many more did so than are recorded in the following chapters. Others are from times when I lived in the countries described. I ran out of print and page space rather than remembered fishing trips. But it was never intended to make this book a lexicon of world fishing. For most of my working life I had to take it where I found it, and was uncommonly glad to do so, as I hope these pages will testify. Possibly because of all the world's oceans my favourite is the Pacific, I have limited inclusion to those tales of fishing around that vast area increasingly labelled the Pacific Rim. But, as will be made clear, this is no fishing guide book to piscatorial delights, hotspots, or necessarily the best fishing to be found around the rim.

Neither are these tales of the very best of the fishing that came my way. I experienced much more exciting and (in terms of the catch) rewarding fishing in other times and other places. But these are about some of those I perhaps best and most fondly remember. There is no chronology in the following chapters. They were put in the following sequence and order to provide a mix rather than a calendar.

Similarly there is no geographical unity or thread linking

up the sequence of chapters. My fishing was often done wherever my sea voyaging took me. My fly rod was usually at the ready, wherever I went. And if there was no trout fishing – even if the ship was then perhaps in the middle of the South Pacific Ocean or in some troutless Asian port – I would take out my fly rod, set it together, and handle it, remembering the places it had taken me to.

These tales, mostly of fly-fishing for trout, occasionally for salmon or sea trout, are true tales. Because they are true, and because I am no more than a modestly competent angler, albeit a passionate one, none are stories of the capture of monster, trophy, record trout. Hopefully, a few of the tales will be remembered for memorable fish or, rather more accurately, for memorable days of fishing in some of the loveliest and most enchanted places I have known.

Not all my fishing tales were sneaked in, as it were, on days away from ships. Several happened on longer leaves between voyages, or during the years when I lived in New Zealand.

The events and circumstances described were all real. I have taken the liberty of naming real people and hope none of those who may read of themselves in these pages will be in any way offended. It had been my intention to be guarded in the true naming of certain places, certain streams, and to give them fictitious names in order not to offend a few of my fishing friends. However, as the book progressed, it became clear that in the majority of cases it would be clear to any knowledgeable reader exactly what rivers I had fished. To have plainly identified, say, the Tongariro River, but have laid a red herring in the case of the Kaipo, would have jarred. I chose, instead, to name names, and hope none of my friends' sensibilities will be in any way offended.

Furthermore, let me say from the outset that none of these tales are intended to convey the idea that in their substance and in their happening anything very important was happening. I tend to agree with the late Robert Traver who said that he fished, not because he regarded fishing as being so terribly important but because he suspected that so many of the other concerns of men are equally unimportant – and not nearly so much fun.

If they convey something of the magic of fly-fishing, and of the places my fly rod took me to, then it will be enough.

It goes without saying that certain commentators will say that here is another dull, only-here-for-the-scenery fishing book, with nothing the reader can learn from it. To such critics I can but reply that there are more than enough of them churning out the same old recycled how-to-do-it stuff to satisfy fishermen whose tastes incline that way.

Most of all, this book is meant to be an entertainment, a diversion in fishing. Nothing more. Extending the vein of diversion, no apology is made for the digressions that sometimes lead these tales of fishing into flights of fancy realms of other-worldliness. If fishing – especially fly fishing for trout – does not sometimes lead its practitioners into such awarenesses, however fleetingly experienced, I can only suggest they are doing it for some of the wrong reasons and missing out on a lot.

Robert Traver, whose sentiments I have already paraphrased, was anything but an only-here-for-the-scenery fisherman. In his *Testament of a Fisherman* he listed a few of the reasons why he fished. You will note that he included such reasons as the taste of bourbon drunk out of an old tin cup – but he also added that maybe one day he might even catch a mermaid:

> **I fish because I love to; because I love the environs where trout are found, which are invariably beautiful, and hate the environs where crowds of people are found, which are invariably ugly; because of all the television commercials, cocktail parties, and assorted social posturing I thus escape; because, in a world where most men seem to spend their lives doing things they hate, my fishing is at once an endless source of delight and an act of small rebellion; because trout do not lie or cheat and cannot be**

bought or bribed or impressed by power, but respond only to quietude and humility and endless patience; because I suspect that men are going along this way for the last time, and I for one don't want to waste the trip; because mercifully there are no telephones on trout waters; because only in the woods can I find solitude without loneliness; because bourbon out of an old tin cup always tastes better out there; because maybe one day I will catch a mermaid; and, finally, not because I regard fishing as being so terribly important but because I suspect that so many of the other concerns of men are equally unimportant – and not nearly so much fun.

At least some of the following tales of fishing are straight-forward enough. But, in others, the reader's forbearance is asked for in the web of frequent digression.

My only defence against that charge is that fishing itself is an endless series of almost ritualised digressions. What begins as the angler's cast – fly line curling and uncurling backwards and forwards through the air as if by some magic – might soon become enthrallment and a sudden detachment at the sight of a kingfisher darting across the stream, or the sound of the plaintive cuckoo in the nearby copse. Clouds, weather, wind and rain, sounds, thoughts, memories and dreams are only a few of the byways of digression familiar to everyone who has moved beyond the mere technicalities of fishing. Here then are some of mine.

Bryn Hammond

8

PROLOGUE:
THE WAY OF A FISHERMAN

In the *Tao Te Ching* Lao Tzu described a Golden Age when man returns to Nature. He announced this as an ideal; something towards which men might strive; but in so doing hinted that few would make the journey. The idea has had many resonances in Chinese literature. Perhaps the most beautiful is the fable of 'The Well in the Peach Blossom Forest', by Tao Yuang-Ming.

Going fishing – the very act of going fishing – is always, for some fishermen at least, a journeying of sorts into another world, a different world from that they normally inhabit. The tales that follow in this book are at one level tales of fishing, but at another level are sometimes tales of journeyings, stumblings, into other worlds.

None are the stuff of high adventure, although many may describe such journeying in faraway places. None of the fishing itself is all that spectacular or even singular, and absolutely none of it is heroic. Hopefully, however, some of these tales will take the reader behind that veil of everyday reality into that world all fishermen are seeking to find, and sometimes, briefly, fleetingly, seem to enter.

Maybe Tao Yuang-Ming's legendary tale comes close to describing that other world fishermen – even like ourselves – sometimes blunder into, or even in and out of, unknowingly:

In the time of Tai Yuan, there lived a fisherman in

9

Wuling. One day he travelled upstream along a
river. He had forgotten whether he had gone near
or far when a great forest, hundreds of yards deep,
and aglow with peach blossoms, appeared on either
side of the river. There were no other trees in the
forest, only beautiful fresh, scented grass, into which
the peach petals fell. The fisherman was amazed
and travelled onward, for he wanted to know where
the forest would end.

At the edge of the forest stood the mountain from
which the river flowed. A narrow entrance led into
the mountain itself, which looked as though it was
surrounded by light. The fisherman walked into
this entrance, following a straight path; but after a
few steps it became light and wide, and a broad,
spreading land lay before his eyes.

Neat huts and tidy houses stood among good
fields and beautiful, shallow waters. Paths crossed
one another; there were all kinds of bamboo, and
many mulberry trees; chickens and dogs answered
one another from village to village. Men and women
sowed the fields – just as it is with us. Children and
old folk were peaceful and serene in what they were
doing.

The people were astonished when they saw our
fisherman, and questioned him eagerly. As he
talked, they gave him wine to drink and slaughtered
chickens for a meal. The villagers heard about it
all, and everyone gathered to ask him questions.
They told him their own tale of how, long ago in the
turbulent times of Qin Shi Huang, their ancestors
had left and come to this place – women, children
and all the people. Since that time no one had ever
gone back, and so they knew nothing of people outside. They asked who was king. They did not know
the dynasty of Han, much less the Wei and the Jin.

But the fisherman brought them tidings of all he knew, and they listened to him. He passed many a day in this manner, feasted and entertained with food and wine. When the time came for them to part, the villagers thought it would not be worthwhile to tell the people outside about it all.

Finally, the fisherman left this land, returned to the river, and stepped into his boat. He remembered the place and its surroundings well. Back in the district capital, he reported to the official, who sent out messengers on the strength of the fisherman's report. However they lost their way . . . .

It is true that later Liu Ji Qi, 'the Wise Man of the South', went boldly forth to search for the place. But before getting there he fell ill and died. Since then no one has asked the way.

This book then may have sufficient of the shades of that old fisherman's report to have made the writing of it worthwhile, both for those who have made similar journeyings, and those who do so vicariously.

THUNDERING ATHABASCA OF
THE ANTIPODES

Far away Tongariro! Green-white thundering
Athabasca River of New Zealand! I vowed I would
come again down across the vast Pacific, and bring
my boy Romer and my brother R.C., to fish in the
swift cold waters of this most beautiful and famous
of trout streams. It is something to have striven. It
is much to have kept your word.
           Zane Grey, *Tales from a Fisherman's Log*, 1978

It is commonplace of recent times when said that everyone
remembers exactly where they were and what they were
doing when they first heard news of the assassination of John
Fitzgerald Kennedy, President of the United States of
America. Even more to the point, they do. In my own case I
was sitting in a bar in Genoa, supposedly warming myself in
an interlude in a brisk walk from the more elegant streets
around the Via XX Settembre, through the narrow streets of
the ancient town, towards the port where my ship was
berthed. It was a cold late November evening; much colder
than that part of the Italian coast normally experiences so
early in the winter. A flurry of snow had fallen in late afternoon. It froze where it fell, and the cobbled streets were icily
slippery.

I sat in this small, typically Genoese bar/restaurant somewhere near the Via Antonio Gramsci, quietly, watching and being watched. A waiter hovered in the doorways leading to the kitchen; behind the bar counter the Patrone sat on a high stool, hugely enveloping and overhanging the seat itself. Bangled arms crossed over a massive, heaving bosom, ever attentive to the few sparse clientele, but nevertheless keeping up a steady flow of banter and repartee with the puttana sitting alone at the table nearest the bar, taking occasional tiny sips from the glass of sambuca in front of her. Once, shortly after I had walked into the place and taken a seat, the puttana had risen from her chair and crossed to my table to invite me to join her at a nearby hotel for an hour of pneumatic sexual bliss. She had once – not even very long ago – been a good-looking woman. Now her once natural blondeness had become brassy and brazen and she was well advanced on the road to becoming old, pitifully at odds with her real age. Perhaps thirty.

But Italian whores – at least those of Genoa – are not a persistent lot and are generally extraordinarily polite. Following my equally polite declining of her proposition she went back to her table, from then on ignoring me, while she engaged in staccato verbal exchanges with the Patrone behind the bar. There were a few other people present, not many: some eating; some drinking. It was, as is especially noticeable in Italy, that time of day best described as indeterminate, when all of Italy seems, for an hour or so, suspended in time.

I had been aware of the muted sound of a radio somewhere behind the bar. It had somehow blended into the overall sound pattern of the place. Suddenly, it was as if there had been an explosion: the Patrone fell off her stool; the waiter rushed into the bar; a customer leapt to his feet, napkin waving, stuffing pasta back into his mouth, from whence it was escaping. There was a babble of voices, a cacophony of sound: all of which was unintelligible to me, except that I somehow knew as if by instinct that a catastrophe had happened, and that it was being even then reported on the radio.

13

It was an odd situation. People came hurrying in from the street. Something serious had happened. The Patrone came round the bar towards me, squeezing in her ample bosoms as she advanced, and I swear she was crying. In excited broken English she told me that President Kennedy was dead – shot, she said, by a bandit – and that he had died in his wife's arms.

Not only did the bar hurriedly empty, but once outside, struggling into my coat, it seemed that Genoa was emptying itself, as if everyone was hurrying home. It was but a short walk back to the Ponte Parodi and I remember thinking how ironic it was, that I had walked by the house where Cristoforo Colombo was born and that, had he not 'discovered' America, maybe there would have been no John F. Kennedy to assassinate four hundred and seventy one years later.

I remember, too, how certain events – and this was one of them – have a sudden illogical effect on people and places many thousands of miles away. As I walked along the Ponte Ethiopa it was apparent that the longshoremen on all the ships in port had decided to stop work, and go home. Even reflecting that dockers everywhere require very little incentive or reason before they stop work, I was still aware, even before getting back to my ship, and hearing the news in more detail from the Voice of America and the BBC, that this sort of thing was probably happening all around the world; that it was a worldwide reaction no one might have anticipated.

In this respect, I believe it to be generally true that the vast majority of people can and do remember exactly where they were, and what they were doing, when they first heard the news that Kennedy had beem mortally shot in Dallas.

In a somewhat similar fashion – and this is not meant to be in any way frivolous, but rather to suggest that certain happenings along our voyage through life, are hard enough and singular enough to etch themselves indelibly in our mind's eye, so that the entire event as it occurred to us at that particular time is triggered by any future reference to it . . . in somewhat similar fashion, I now suggest, no one ever seems to forget the

14

time, the exact place, and the circumstances, when they caught their first ever fresh-run rainbow trout from New Zealand's Tongariro River. Most people can remember the first trout they caught, but afterwards events seem to blur very much one into another, except perhaps for the most assiduous keepers of fishing diaries. And even among them, I suspect, there have been many lapses, if the truth were known, so that the fishing events of one day somehow become transported to another, and that the fishing recollected as having been in one particular place, happened in fact in another.

But for New Zealanders themselves, as well as for all the visiting fly-fishermen I've ever known, the circumstances of the capture of their first ever Tongariro trout are forever etched in their minds – rather than simply among their memories. Mine, at least, was no different. It happened so:

The river has its periods of suffering from changing fashion, but by and large the Tongariro is, and remains, the most famous trout stream in the world, and for many, incontrovertibly, the best.

In my case I had fly fished some tumbling mountain streams around the snow-capped and perfect volcanic cone of Mount Egmont in Taranaki. I had already fished Lake Tutira, near Napier, on the opposite coast of the North Island, as well as a few Hawkes Bay rivers, but the Tongariro was still a place of dreams I had only read and heard about.

'Far away Tongariro!' wrote Zane Grey. 'Green-white thundering Athabasca River of New Zealand,' he had called it. But, apart from Grey, I had read everything I could lay my hands on about this famous river, longing for the actuality of travelling there and fishing its hallowed waters.

Then one day quite out of the blue my friend Alan Bowes visited me in the ship at Napier and said, 'How about a few days fishing at Taupo? Any chance of you getting away first thing tomorrow morning?' It was not only possible, but I jumped at it!

Next day, before most of Napier was rising out of sleep, Alan and I were heading northwards from the town, then soon away westwards on the old road through the Esk Valley, up and over the high central volcanic plateau towards Taupo. Today the road is good, but in those days it was still something of an adventure. Alan, a splendid fly fisherman, is one of that breed of New Zealanders to whom a gadget called a Volcano is an essential part of going anywhere, and we had hardly cleared beyond Te Pohue hill before he stopped the car to brew up the first mug of tea. A Volcano is a single-piece con-struction of steel consisting of an inner container for water accessed via a short wide spout, then at the bottom of the water chamber a wide steel skirt with large holes cut into it for fuel in the shape of bits of newspaper and a few loose twigs, both to be inserted, ignited, and made to boil the water in an incredibly short time. Tea made from Volcano-boiled water, with a few twigs of manuka for fuel, has the most delicious, smokey yet subtle and exotic flavour, yet takes no more than a few minutes.

Although I was eager to get to Taupo and be fishing, it was good to stop along the road and savour the prospect through the aroma and unique pungency of Volcano-brewed tea. The day was crisp and clear, with that startling clarity of air and sky unique to the high country of New Zealand. It was the very end of September, not quite the beginning of spring, and the breeze had an edge to it disarmingly cold, although shel-tered from it by the merest low tussock of near alpine grasses, the sun had welcome warmth.

Another brew of tea beneath the Mohaka River road bridge and we were on our way towards Taupo and what, for me at least, was to be crystallized as being the green-white thunder-ing Athabasca River – the Tongariro.

At last we drove over the lip of the hill that suddenly yields the first full unfolding view of Lake Taupo that lay in shim-mering sun-dappled magnificence before us. Little did I think that several years later I would come to live on that as yet still undeveloped shore across Tapuaeharuru Bay from Acacia Bay on the western side to Rangatira Point.

Taupo was still a sleepy, small, pumice-dusty, frontier-like sort of town. Alan diverted a little way to drive through what there was of a town. He stopped the car along what is now Lake Terrace. There was a fenced off area of scrubby bush and manuka scrub, all ghostly white with pumice dust from the unmade roads, and at the front of it a painted notice, itself thick with pumice (and pumice dust makes whatever it settles on look very old and uncared for), announcing that large sections (the New Zealand term for a house building plot) were for sale at £100 each. Alan said, 'Why don't you buy one, Bryn? Invest a little in New Zealand's future!' Today this stretch of the Lake Taupo foreshore is occupied by a long line of shoulder-to-shoulder multi-million dollar hotels and motor lodges.

A quick call at the town's then only tackle shop to buy our Taupo District fishing licences and invest a little money wisely in a few Taupo flies and invaluable up-to-the-minute intelligence of the fishing, and we were soon off again, heading southwards down the eastern lakeshore. Alan had decided to stay at Jack Neill's Fishing Lodge at Te Rangi-Ita rather than in Turangi itself. He was a regular here, and the choice a good one, although as we unpacked into our separate wooden cabins and Alan suggested we put up our rods and walk down the short distance to the mouth of the Tauranga-Taupo River where it entered the lake, I was only impatient to press on to the magic Tongariro River itself.

I was surprised at how small and insignificant looking the mouth of the Tauranga-Taupo really was, although the scene, looking out across the wide, sunlit lake, was breathtaking. Alan led to the water's edge, stripping off line as he paddled ankle deep in the gently swirling water lapping up over a beach of powdered pumice and sand; as unlikely a place to start fly-fishing for trout as I had ever previously encountered – or so I thought.

He cast the fly outwards across the stream water entering the lake; short casts, hardly more than chucks, almost as if he was practicing before getting down to something more serious. Then, calling me over his shoulder, he told me to move in ahead of him.

Suddenly, his rod tip bowed almost double and his reel screeched as the hooked fish stripped off fly line as it headed out across the lake. He couldn't have been fishing for more than a minute! With such practised dexterity it seemed to me to border on nonchalance he soon played and beached his fish: a fat rainbow hen of exactly five pounds. Then, while I hooked and lost two fish in quick succession, Alan hooked and beached four more – all between three and five pounds – in the next half hour. With an almost arrogant self-confidence he said he wanted to get a few quick ones into Jack Neill's smokehouse. Then he apologized for this diversion. 'Come on,' he said. 'Let's get you down to the Tongariro!'

We left our fly rods made up just as they were, putting them in the rod holders on the car, both still wearing thigh waders, for the short journey southwards on through Turangi to the Tongariro. Just a matter of minutes, and as we crossed over the main highway bridge I saw the green-white thundering Athabasca waters for the first time.

For my introduction to the Tongariro Alan had decided to take me to the Major Jones Pool. As hundreds of other anglers have done – and I since, too, a hundred times – we parked the car at the end of Koura Street, took down our fly rods, and crossed the wooden footbridge to the true right bank of the river. Far below us the crystal clear water, albeit it was green-white and thundering, cascaded down from the Breakfast Pool above, then down into the wider, quieter water of the Major Jones Pool itself. As we crossed over the bridge I could see perhaps six fishermen working the pool below. Some were chest-deep in the old Tongariro fashion – just a pair of shoulders, a black japara parka-covered head above, and two arms held high: one wielding the fly rod; the other controlling the sweeping water-searching fly line and fly. A few were fishing closer in, barely knee deep, although in the universal manner of the day it was all downstream fishing with a Taupo lure on a fast sinking line, cast out and across, then allowed to sweep around in the current until it hung directly downstream before being twitched back in a figure-of-eight hand coiling before being cast again.

There was an almost balletic convention in those days of well-mannered Taupo-style fly-fishing. At the end of each cast every angler would step a few yards downstream. One entered a line of anglers at the top of a pool, waiting until there was sufficient space for one to get in and begin casting without bothering or cramping the style of the man ahead in the next downstream position. On reaching the bottom of the pool being fished each angler waded out of the water on to the riverbank, then walked upstream out of the way of the anglers fishing down the pool, before re-entering from the top and starting the process all over again.

On this, my first day on what seemed to me to be the holy of holies, there proved to be only three or four others actually fishing as we approached the head of the pool through the well-worn bush track leading to the river clearing. It meant that Alan and I were able to wade straight into the top lie and begin casting. He tried to insist that I went ahead of him, but I was too much in awe of the place for that, so I fished about ten or twelve yards behind and upstream of him. I can clearly remember the sense of occasion I felt – almost as if I had been admitted to an exclusive club – but that I was being watched, to see if I warranted admission into these mystic rites.

I had (at least in my own mind) passed that point along the route of my apprenticeship in fly-fishing in gleaning a little discernment in the matter of tackle; at least in the ways I then perceived it. Until a year or so before this time I had been amply satisfied with my one and only fly rod: a nine-foot hollow fibreglass and excellent American rod made by Eagle Claw. I had bought it in Seattle, and it had done me well, until

I fell foul of that snobbery of fishing tackle which besets most anglers in their beginning years.

I had become convinced that what I really needed was a quality split cane fly rod from Hardy's. Yes, it had to be a Hardy rod, and I wouldn't listen to the several helpful and honest tackle salesmen who suggested there were a few other equally good manufacturers. But I would have none of it. My reading and gut feelings told me that nothing but a Hardy split cane fly rod would be good enough: not just not good enough for me, ran my thinking, but not good enough for the hallowed, almost sacred trout waters I was going to fish.

Lest anyone ridicule these sentiments – foolish though they are – if you care to think about it, then most fly fishermen pass through such a phase. Oppositely, however, another type of angler persists in going on using, year after year, a fly rod, reel, and fly line that by rights should have been long ago consigned to the local dump. Such are the strange byways along the fly fisherman's path!

Needless to say, in the matter of equipping myself with a pedigreed fly rod a few months earlier, it was to be a Hardy. This, of course, was long before the days of carbonfibre and boron, and in my ignorance I did not realise how good the best glass rods were; my own proven Eagle Claw rod included. In those particular days even split cane rods were in short supply, but there before me in the racks were two that tempted me sorely. One was a Hardy L.R.H. No.2; the other a Hardy Rogue River. The L.R.H. would no doubt have been the most suitable rod for my needs, but the very sound of the name 'Rogue River' really sold it to me.

After all, wasn't I going to fish the fabled Tongariro River in the footsteps of Zane Grey? And did not the very sound of the L.R.H. as being a dry fly rod make it far too wandlike and delicate for the heavy, big-fish usage I would put it to?

And that, approximately, is how I came to have a Hardy Rogue River split cane fly rod on that very first day on the Tongariro. As for the reel, I was still sticking with my trusted

American Pfleuger Medallist – in those days a badge of excellence in New Zealand – because it was tremendously strong and held an enormous length of backing behind a fast sinking fly line – a security of which I was constantly certain I would need most desperately the very next time out.

The reader, I hope, will forgive yet another diversionary intrusion in this tale. I am not an angling technician, but in recounting this story of my first Tongariro rainbow trout, and because of the sense of occasion that came with the event, I consider it only right and proper to describe with just what tackle the deed was done: that in my Rogue River fly rod, Medallist reel, and Wet Cel fly line, I was suitably equipped for the unique occasion.

We fished down through about half the length of the Major Jones. I remember being abreast the old tower on the opposite bank and wondering whether time had come to change from the Hamill's Killer fly I had on, when suddenly, towards the end of the across and downstream traverse of my fly I felt a sudden bump – as if the fly had hit an underwater boulder and lodged in it – then suddenly the fly line tautened and thrummed like a double bass string, throwing off droplets of water in a kaleidoscopic cascade of prismic colour in the late afternoon slanting sunlight. With an explosion of water the fish made one, two, three, great surging leaps into the air, heading away upstream as if it was determined to complete its spawning journey.

After a searing run upstream until it was directly opposite me the fish then hung under the overhang of the far bank, tugging and thrumming away like mad, and with a fury and strength I had never before experienced. Then, taking me completely by surprise, it suddenly spun round and turned downstream, racing beyond all power of halting, and I let it go. At this juncture I thought it meant to return to the lake, a few miles downstream. With what to me seemed an alarming amount of backing beyond the rod tip – but probably no more than ten or twenty yards – the hooked fish came across the

21

shallower water far too close for my liking to two anglers wading deep at the bottom of the pool.

No sooner had I tentatively tested the bend of the rod and what I considered to be some judicious pumping, and had begun to regain some line back on to the reel and feel more in charge of events, than the rainbow streaked off upstream again. What with a belly of slack line, curved between me and the fish in the heavy, roily downstream flow, for what seemed a frighteningly long time I lost all tactile contact with the trout. At the very moment when I began to doubt whether, in fact, it was still there, it took off again, leading me a merry dance trying to follow it – Tongariro boulders are like underwater cannon balls – until time took its toll and by sheer good luck and the last of its tremendous upstream-downstream runs the fish began to tire; its runs shortened and became less frenetic, and I was able to gain more line than was ever subsequently lost again. I was also able to back out of the river on to safer ground until the end was in sight. Four, five, maybe six times, however, I overestimated that benign moment and sought to shorten line so much that I could see the fish hanging in and across the current only yards beyond the rod tip.

Landing nets can be an abomination on the Tongariro unless a trout is to be released, but this one was meant to be a keeper, and I intended to beach it in true Tongariro fashion. But on this occasion, at that time, the trout had no intention of coming in that easily. After a heart-stopping surge and flurry in the shallower water opposite me, it took off again, back to midstream and the heavier flow, against which it hung, fighting for its life.

There were three or four such last surges of power, but the histrionics and gymnastics were over. Even in those days, such was almost always a sad sort of moment for me. Somehow, as long as there remains a good chance that the fish can make its escape and survive, I am half-hoping it will throw the hook and do so; however sad and awful the loss will seem. For there is perhaps nothing better for an angler's soul than to see, at such a moment, the fly come away with a last shake of the head, and a big trout turn away, turn its back on the angler, and streak off to its proper domain.

Despite such fleeting thoughts even then, this was no such occasion. My sole intention was to beach and kill this first Tongariro rainbow trout. When at last I guided it high and dry on to the pebbled, sandy bank of the Major Jones Pool on that particular day, it seemed like a dream come true.

As I knelt to remove the fly – stuck, it seemed to me, so delicately and so loosely in the tissue right in the scissors of its jaw – and grasped it firmly at the wrist of the tail, I could feel a trembling last surge of great power. But I still took out my priest and killed it there and then, cleanly and well, but still with a sort of sadness and regret in having killed something so beautiful.

But this was my first Tongariro trout. It lay there on the wet sand at my feet: a gorgeously arrayed and splendid maiden fresh-run rainbow hen of four pounds. At that moment my very pride and joy!

Since that first day I have known the Tongariro well, over many years and seasons, and in many pools and runs much more to my liking than the Major Jones Pool. Even up to that time of my introduction to it, the Major Jones was considered to be the finest pool on the river, and the river to be the finest trout stream in the world. Many is the time that better fishermen than I will ever be have lost fish, fly, fly line, and a hundred or more yards of stout backing on the first wild downstream run of a taking rainbow in the Major Jones. One morning, a few years later, I arrived there, waiting to go in at the head of the pool, and recognised the renowned Vice-Admiral Harold Hickling beginning to fish through the water. He was right up in the neck, just below the rapids, when a rainbow took his fly and almost took the rod out of his hands. It raced downstream like greased lightning, and kept on going, stripping off an entire brand new heavy fly line, then exactly one hundred yards of equally brand new backing. He was in a dilemma. He couldn't follow the fish downstream, as often can be done in the Tongariro, because from where he had waded out there was nowhere to go. Within a matter of seconds it was all over. The Admiral had lost fish, fly, fly line, backing, through something inevitable rather than from any fault of his own.

It happened to me once, twenty years later, but further upstream in the river at Harry's Rock when a similar rainbow trout took my small Hare's Ear nymph, and kept on going, and it wasn't entirely due to my bungling incompetence. I stood there in the shallows just below Harry's Rock. The fish, hooked in the deep run alongside the far righthand bank, simply turned in the current with the nymph in its mouth, hooked itself, and kept on going. It went past me, barely a few yards away, while I vainly tried to gather in slack line and make some sort of contact again. It came all too soon, and there was suddenly no slack for me to gather, but the line was tearing out off the reel, burning my fingers, and then the backing, until it was all gone, trailing after the fish heading outwards towards Lake Taupo. Luckily I had the wit to point the rod tip at the departing fish before the crunch came. I watched the last few turns of backing peel off the reel spool. Then there was a sudden tension, and a little puff of what seemed all the world like smoke from the spool and the line parted and the running rainbow trout continued on its own majestic journey unencumbered by my unwelcome intrusion upon it – albeit still towing a hundred and thirty four yards of my tackle behind it.

Of such stuff are the best of fishing days remembered.

KANGAROOS AND RAINBOW
TROUT AT DEE LAGOON

> Some circumstantial evidence is very strong, as
> when you find a trout in the milk.
>
> Henry David Thoreau

With no wish to enter into a discussion about past and present modes of deep sea international shipping, there can be no doubt that the old had a charm and romance about it, while the new is inconceivably dull – and takes longer, too. The time of which I write was not, in fact, so very long ago, but it was before the world-wide revolution of container shipping, then of dubious flags of convenience. It is now euphemistically described as being a period of de-regulation and international adjustment.

The British Conference Lines serving Australia and New Zealand had their share of critics even before then, and may have deserved much of that criticism, but by and large they served the maritime interests of those countries, and of the world in general, well. Suffice it to say, in opening another chapter in a book such as this, that they operated often exceedingly fast and regular liner services in the carriage of outward and homeward cargoes, as well as passengers, and positioned their ships in the ports of both antipodean countries in sufficient numbers, capabilities, and sequence, to be able to load all the seasonal refrigerated and chilled cargoes, as they became available, and carrying them, as required, to the four corners of a far-flung world.

For the purposes of this present tale – set in the island State of Tasmania – as many as were called for of the Conference Lines ships would be there at the ports of Hobart, Beauty Point and Launceston, to load the apple crop, as well as the lesser tonnages of pears. Despite being seasonal the apple harvest was sometimes late, or delayed by inclement weather, or certain essential varieties and grades of apples might only be harvested a week or two after a main crop of some more popular variety.

As a consequence of this, what might otherwise have been a week or a fortnight of loading, could be spread over a month – even more. Additionally, the Australian waterside worker was an independent character who liked to be back in the nearest pub by a few minutes after 5 pm on working days (in those days the pubs closed at 6 pm, so there was not much time for serious drinking); and on Saturdays and Sundays they worked not at all. In fact there wasn't a great deal of time in between in which to load the huge ships, but somehow, slowly, each in turn would complete loading and head off east across the Pacific, or west across the Indian or Southern Ocean, to destinations in Europe and Asia, and a hundred other wayports en route.

As a very final digression before getting on with my tale of fishing, it might be as well to explain that on the particular voyage of the particular ship of which I now write, we were to load a full cargo of apples for discharge at Hamburg, Antwerp and London, but were to make the voyage via Aden, Jeddah, and the Suez Canal. The reason: the ship had been booked to carry a fairly large consignment of apples to Jeddah in Saudi Arabia. The variety of apple chosen was by long custom, for these were not to be stored in chilled refrigerator storage chambers at Jeddah, but simply discharged from the ship on to the open quay, then straightaway loaded on to the backs of open road trucks. From there, we were told, the trucks would speed along the dusty, hot, arid, Jeddah to Mecca road, where the apples would be sold to the countless groups of countless pilgrims making their way – mostly on foot – on the Haj to the holy city. Not, mark you, selling apples by the pound or kilo, but in cut quarters – that is one quarter of a single apple.

With luck and the utmost despatch the first trucks away from the port might catch up with the first roadside bands of tired, hungry, thirsty pilgrims along the desert road and be selling them a cut slice of a juicy Tasmanian apple even before the chilled cool of the ship's refrigeration plant had been exchanged for the burning heat of the Arabian sands. And on this particular voyage my ship was even further held up in Hobart awaiting this specific consignment of apples for Saudi Arabia.

Being a trout fisherman I don't think the delay bothered me too much. The local manager of our shipping agency in Tasmania responded to the sight of fishing books lying around my dayroom and, although not a trout fisherman himself, suggested that a friend of his would be interested to meet me and talk about the available fishing.

That evening I received a visit from Alan Henry whose job led him everywhere across the enormous tangled web of hydro-electric and water-impoundment developments throughout the central highlands of the island. He was also the sort of man who kept his fly-fishing tackle always there, always ready, in the back of his station wagon. Within minutes he invited me to join him for a few days fishing in one of the central, high country lakes and associated streams. He suggested perhaps another two from the ship might like to come along, and the two people I had in mind were delighted with the prospect.

We set out next day. It was the last day of April, with a chill already in the air down on the coast at Hobart. Alan had a trailer-boat in tow – he told us that, as we would see, some of the places we were going to fish were really only accessible by boat.

27

We were heading for Dee Lagoon, and we were going to stay at the lakeside hut belonging to the Hobart Fly Tyers' Club. Just to be going fishing again was enough, but I somehow knew that this was going to be something unique in the way of fishing trips.

Our journey inland took us along the Derwent Valley and into the Central Highlands, skirting the wet, near rain forests of the entirely rugged southwest of the island, and more heading into the harder, hardier, sclerophyll forests of the centre. There were several deviations along the way, and by the time we had climbed into the highland region the air was cooling fast. There would be a sharp frost tonight.

Twilight was already darkening the eastern sky across the waters of the lake. We turned off the road, and after some tortuous tracks through the stands of myrtles, pencil pines, and eucalypts, came into a leafy glade where stood the hut of the Hobart Fly Tyers; a wooden cabin, pleasingly primitive and old, standing back twenty or so yards from the lake edge. The ground was thick with crunchy sheddings of a hundred trees that canopied the hut like a vast umbrella: leaves, twigs, pine needles, the shredded bark of gums, and the sound of one's footsteps through it was almost hostile and alien to the abiding natural quiet of the place.

Alan, our host, was a well organised man. He soon had us all engaged in the very first ritual to be attended to; the gathering up, while there was twilight left, to gather up wood for the fire in the hut. There was a great pile of such wood already stacked just outside the door, but it was explained to us that users of the hut were required by ritual to renew the stocks left by the previous occupants even before they began to burn that which had been left for them. And as the night wore on, and the sharp frost descended about Dee Lagoon, I would learn that the very welcome iron stove fire would consume great quantities of wood.

After that we carried in our gear and food supplies, while Alan got the fire going and lit the old hurricane lamps. It was very much a real backwoods hut, with few pretensions towards comfort and modern living, but bliss after the sharp angularities and steel and formica and unnatural brightness of a large modern ship. There were four plain bunks, four chairs, a deal table, a few basic utensils, and little else.

Having the lust and greed for fishing that I do – or at least still had in those days – I had somehow assumed that our first priority would be to set up our fly rods and begin fishing as soon as possible. But Alan had already announced that Dee Lagoon was no place to fish after dark, and that there were other far more basically important things to do. My companions agreed with him, and they set about firing up the second, cooking stove, sorting out the huge steaks we had brought along, and otherwise preparing for what was to be more of a primitive feast than a simple meal. I would have to wait until next day to start fishing.

Good Scotch in tin mugs takes on superlative subtleties of flavour and taste in such places and surroundings. I swear it was the finest whisky I have ever drunk. A sufficiency of it was drunk while the steaks grilled to add a not unpleasing glow to both the surroundings and the occasion. The lamplight and the flickering, dancing shadows that wove from them about the smoke stained rough cut plank walls did much to weave a spell around us, and even before we began what turned out to be a delectable meal, the banter and talk grew better after each refilling of our whisky mugs.

When the eating was done and satiety spread around the table there was a quietly relaxed air. Earlier on Alan had told us where the camp loo was situated – a wooden dunny of recognisably Australian outback construction and type to be found about a hundred yards along the track to one side of the hut. He had said, somewhat jocularly I'd thought, to be a little wary when using it at night, as it seemed to hold a great attraction for the kangaroos and wallabies that abounded thereabouts.

In our now relaxed post-prandial near torpid ease, the fire

blazed and heated the hut marvellously; its fiery tongues and curling shadows of swirling smoke reflected from the cabin walls like a magic lantern show. The effect of such comfort and sense of well-being, as well as the magic of the whisky, drunk as it should be drunk, in quiet companionship, had eased the hearts and minds of all of us, and the talk became reminiscent – men telling tales of amusing incidents in their outdoors, fishing lives – all very relaxed.

At about that time I waited for one of Gerry's cautionary tales to end, then announced that nature called, and I was about to seek out the dunny. I picked up my torch because by now it was pitch black outside. As I got to the door of the hut and was about to open it and go outside, Alan called out to me, "Watch out for the kangaroos. They're certain to come after you!", but in such a manner I was sure it was nothing but a joke played on all first-time visitors.

Outside the night was cold – unbelievably cold, I thought, after such a mild and often sunny day. The barely discernible path led through a great and ancient avenue of tall trees, rustling in the night breeze, with that almost mysterious sound that only comes from the wind in eucalypts, when even the hanging fronds of peeling ghost bark sound more reminiscent of ancient Buddhist temples than the Australian bush. Underfoot the age-old aggregate of the ceaseless debris of a living forest crunched a different, harsher, human-made sound. I flashed my torch from side to side, seeking ahead to locate my destination. Overhead the tall trees rustled their nightsong, and through their topmost branches I could see the cold night glitter of a myriad of stars. As always I looked for the great constellation of Orion, because I feel at home with it above, and always look to see those familiar stars whenever and wherever I find myself enjoying something memorable. As I looked overhead, upwards through the only partly veiling canopy of trees, I remembered that Orion would be beyond the western horizon, but close towards the constellation's outer edges I could make out and immediately recognises the reddish glow of Canopus and, bearing away to the south, down the lake, the familiar pattern of Crux, the Southern Cross.

Then, ahead of me and a little to one side, I saw the dunny. It was the prototype of the real Australian bush dunny, so well constructed many years past from stout native timbers, but now so old that time itself had taken a hand and begun to re-absorb the edifice back into the dreamtime before its begin-nings. In other words the whole thing leaned over like the Leaning Tower of Pisa. The lean-to roof seemed intact, but moss-covered and liana-like suckers entwined it. The door was slightly ajar and the top hinge was broken. It was, in fact, holding itself up. Inside it was as basic as could possibly be, but had the essential of a fixed wooden seat with a hole in the middle leading downwards into the earth.

It was possible to lift the broken door so that I could gain entry, then – by scraping out with my boot a big pile up of leaves – it was possible to at least partly close the door. At least it kept out most of the cold night air – albeit it passed through my mind that the very act of closing the door was a strangely prim, oddly euphemistic act out here in the Tasmanian bush. With that I then shone my torch around the dunny interior and made preparations for the basic functional purpose intended.

Once seated and about this essential business I fell to mus-ing (as one does at such times) about the incredible diversity of such conveniences I had known in various parts of the world, from primitive to positively palatial.

There were night noises, faint whirrings, the sound of wind waves rippling on the nearby lakeshore. Once, I thought I may have heard a bird-call, perhaps an owl, but the night nois-es were, I thought, overlaid one on top of the other, something like an orchestra in the last stages of tuning up, when differ-ent instruments may utter brief phrases, snatches, of melody, before tuning again on some sustained note.

And then, once again much in the way that dunnies – even ones such as I now occupied – cause one to muse on unex-

31

pected things, my mind wandered off about the nature of sounds: what they were; whether sounds were happenings, had reality, in themselves, as it were; or no more than singularly regarded and interpreted inside our own heads as brain processes, signals coming from afar. something in the manner of a radio. I had been recently reading, and fused on elements from two quite different books: both long forgotten, as it happens, although the effects of something from each of them must have triggered off something in my mind that night, sitting in a crude dunny, near a wooden hut in the wilds of Tasmania, I remember well to this day.

I remember wondering if, after all, there were no sounds until there was someone to hear them; more importantly to name them, and by naming them bringing them into existence. After all it was here in Australia that the ancient Aborigines literally sang the world into existence. Whether the world is not determined. Maybe it just isn't 'there' independent of our observation: that, as some would have it, reality is created by the observer. And did those vague sounds of the night have no meaning, or existence, other than waves of frequency of air in motion, other than in my hearing of them. But if this is so, then there are no sounds, and the world is a deathly silent place unless someone is there to hear them. Likewise, the concept goes, that one must imagine a world before there were humans in it. Or imagine a world that had humans in it as yet without the power of speech. Would it then have any meaning to say that birds sang, trees rustled, brooks burbled? Would the sky be sometimes dappled in roseate hues? Were there fish before we said they were? Before we had given the name swimming to what they did in the water, can they, in any sense that matters to us as aestheticians, be said to have swum?

But none were questions as such, or – as far as musings were concerned – of any more import than age-old aids to the processes of defecation, the natural emptying of one's bowels. This slight departure into the realms of quantum mechanics was, however, short-lived, interrupted.

Suddenly, from somewhere close outside, I heard the rustle of movement. Not the rustle of the wind through the trees, or the strange rheumatic creakings of storm-damaged branches, but of ground movements, of moving things on the ground not far outside the door – behind which I not too securely sat. It never occurred to me that it could possibly be anything other than one or two of my companions, who had crept down from the hut and were now about to play a practical joke on me.

There was a rustle and a scuffling right outside the door, then a thump against the outer wall on the right-hand side; then more scuffling in the heavy carpet of decayed leaves and pine needles. This was followed by a banging and crashing outside the opposite wall; the sturdy old timbers resonant with the sound. Then, it was back out front again, alternating between a distinct scuffling around on the soft ground, and an intermittent but deliberate hitting against the wood walls at ground level. I was convinced that one or more of my friends were out there; probably with a stick with which they were scraping through the fallen leaves, or hitting against the wooden walls of the dunny.

With a show of bravado that seemed false even to me, sitting inside with my trousers down around my ankles, I called out, "I know you're out there! Don't be so bloody silly and let me be in peace."

There was silence. I called out again. This time it brought an immediate response. There was a fearful kicking right behind me at the back, outside the dunny, so fierce it seemed to me the whole thing might collapse on top of me. But still I did not think otherwise than I was being the butt of a prank played upon me by my companions.

Nevertheless, I got to my feet, performing the final part of the ritual with more haste than was perhaps wise or hygienic, and pulled up my trousers. Outside, the banging and clattering continued, if anything with increased insistence. Standing up inside this shrine there was precious little room between me and the door – which opened inwards. Squeezing myself to

33

one side I took hold of the handle in one hand, and my electric torch in the other. With a sudden movement, both lifting the broken door while simultaneously pulling it open, inwards, I switched on the torch – fully expecting to see one of my teasing, slightly inebriated companions outside.

Instead, I came face to face with a kangaroo. I don't know which of us was the most surprised. The kangaroo did not, at first, leap away into the darkness, but sat there on his powerful haunches, one arm raised as if for all the world to knock on the door, just looking at me. In as much disbelief, I thought afterwards, as I was looking at him. The light from my torch came back to me from his dark topaz coloured eyes. Of my human companions, there was no sign. Then I knew the fact of the situation.

It may have seemed interminable: me looking at the kangaroo; the kangaroo looking at me; for it is a scientific fact that alcohol is a depressant and slows down, rather than speeds up, our human responses to events. The fact was that it was brief enough for me not to have time to be frightened or even mildly scared. Not yet, at least. I don't really know how or what I felt in those moments.

But in the necessary moment of timelessness, still with my torchlight shining directly into his eyes, the kangaroo suddenly leapt into action. Hitting the door frame with a boxer-like feint, followed by an almighty kick against the half-open door with a powerful foot while the other leg went into overdrive, the kangaroo bounded off into the night, and in the light of my torch I saw others joining it from nearby – although they may have been extremely large wallabies – as they spread out through the forest night and were gone.

If I wasn't actually frightened at that time, then certainly my heartbeat was racing. With as much decency as possible at such a time I completed my errand, then walked back through the trees towards the flickering lamplight in the cabin window. With as much composure as I could muster I took a deep breath and opened the door, vaguely wondering how best

34

to start my story.

But I needn't have bothered. All my companions were still sitting around the table. It was obvious that none of them had even moved in my absence. The whisky was running well and the room was full of laughter as one of them came to the end of some anecdote. They took no notice of me whatsoever. Then Alan, hearing the door, looked over his shoulder and straight at my face, and he said, "I know. Don't tell us. You were disturbed by a kangaroo! I told you! It happens every time!"

With that I poured myself a drink and told my tale, just as I am now telling it to you.

Next morning we were up and out of our sleeping bags by the time the sun rose above the forest on the other side of the lagoon. A heavy frost rimed inside and out the cabin window. Yesterday's underfoot forest carpet of a million leaves, twigs, and pine needles was white with frost, as if each separate piece and sliver had been painted with a silvery white. The still weak sun edged up over the treetops across the lake. It was a silent morning. The wind had died away altogether.

We dressed and made the usual perfunctory cold morning ablutions; lighting the fire, making tea and cooking a hearty breakfast that belied the amplitude of the previous night's meal. Then, with great savour and expectancy for the day to come, we were off fishing.

Alan, who of course knew the water well, told us that there was little point in fly-fishing from the lagoon shore along that side near the hut. It was late in the season; the brown trout already moving towards their appointed spawning grounds; insect and larval life pulling in on itself before the onset of winter, and even the water snails and other teeming mollusca and arthropods abounding there would already be in quietude, so that the still present rainbow trout would be foraging for whatever food organisms they could get, and be quite unselective.

Instead, we launched the boat and he proposed to drop

each one of us off at selected spots on the far side of the lagoon, from where we could each move around and fly fish from the shore.

Tasmanian Central Highland lakes, as has been said, have only very rarely not been interfered with by man. Much of the entire island seems to be a vast network of hydro-electric schemes and water impoundments yet, strangely, one sees little evidence of the usual bespoiling hand of man. This country is too wild for the imprint of man's works to last long upon it, so that the scars are often softened by the very nature of the often harsh, uncompromising countryside.

One less redeeming feature of man's handiwork on the landscape lies in the ever present vistas of drowned forests. Many of the larger lakes throughout the region were once little more than sub-alpine tarns. As dams were built, and the water levels raised, there was much flooding of adjacent forested land. Trees, like grey ghosts, in various stages of death and decay by drowning, loom up out of the waters of a hundred such enhanced impoundments, where a small natural lake may have been engineered into a large lake, flooding hundreds of acres of forest, or a series of tarns, connected by burns across moorland or through mountain forest may have been turned into a vastly greater single body of controlled water, to be put to use through the great web of penstocks generating vast amounts of electric power.

Only very rarely do huge and spread out hydro-electric developments improve fresh water habitats for trout and salmon, despite what their apologists say. But, in Tasmania, this may have been achieved, in having a vast total project spread out over a huge area of highlands. Only time will tell. Suffice it to say that since the very early introduction of hydro-power schemes in the island State, the quality of both brown and rainbow trout fishing, almost everywhere, has been enhanced. However, as we shall see, the common environmental balance for both species living side by side is almost never achieved for long. Different in their demands, either brown trout or rainbows come to dominate most fisheries, and by raising or lowering water levels the once dominant of the species may be replaced by the other in a dramatic turnaround.

At first, it must be said, the forlorn sight of drowned forests everywhere, with great tree trunks still standing proud, rearing out of the water everywhere one looks, is nothing short of disturbing. It is like something out of another world. But in the same manner that a dammed river valley, flooded for water storage and stocked with introduced trout almost always produces splendid fishing for the early years, so in Tasmania the very extensions of natural lakes and tarns has not only enlarged the trout habitats beyond belief, but made the waters enriched by the best of nutrients and insect and other creature life, almost beyond comprehension. Even more importantly the very nature of the Tasmanian system has created both vast numbers of new spawning streams and rivulets, and huge areas of shallows where brown and rainbow trout can prosper far better than they can in the more usual steep-sided, deep water lakes so created in other countries.

Dee Lagoon is long and narrow at its northern end, but opens up into a more expansive stretch of water some two miles broad and long on its southern and eastern arm. The lagoon is mostly surrounded by beautiful forest and with a static water level is generally considered to be the most picturesque fishery in the Bronte region.

Tasmanian fishing regulations do vary from water to water but, generally speaking, are remarkably tolerant, permitting spinning and trolling as well as fly-fishing. Dee Lagoon is generally considered to be a "difficult" fishery among most local anglers. This may be because few seem to do better than catch one or two trout at the most on most visits; mostly rainbows, although brown trout are present in considerable numbers. Due to the large areas of dense, still standing drowned forest, and the considerable scattering of fallen timber in the shallower parts of the lake, where the trout are mostly concentrated, the fly fisherman has a distinct advantage with his ability to cast into heavily timbered stretches of water, often casting his fly parallel to and close alongside overhanging logs. But the sight of it is somewhat forbidding and the beauty of the place is marred by the standing armies of drowned trees.

On this first outing to the lagoon Alan took the boat to the shallows and weed beds that extend from Moss Banks to Mentmore Bay, dropping each one of us at some convenient wading and casting spot before moving further up into the shallows himself. By now the brown trout would have left the lake for the spawning streams and creeks. If we were to catch anything they would be rainbows.

The fabulous jassid beetle falls that provide the very best of the fly-fishing were over so late now in the season, and all my attempts at interesting a trout in a nymph of any description proved useless. There was no sign of any surface activity that morning, even after the warming sun burned the cold night air from off the water. All, in fact, seemed in vain, as well, as far as I could see, for my companions in the far distance, but the act of fishing itself was, as always, therapeutically good.

It was strange to cast out a line on to the placid lake, to see a platypus suddenly appear in view out there on the water and curve in towards one's fly line, as if to investigate, but then recognise the foreigness of the thing, and sheer off, speeding up in swimming away from it. It was my first experience of fly-fishing for trout among these wild duckbilled platypus that seemed – to me, at least – incongruous on a trout lake, despite the fact that the platypus is indigenous to Australia, while rainbow and brown trout are alien, introduced, acclimatised, and exotic species; the real outlandish foreigners.

In the space of a few hours I had several pulls to let me know there were good trout around, but they somehow seemed all half-hearted. In desperation I tied on a New Zealand Red Setter, changed to a slow sinking line, and was almost immediately fast into a fish that wrapped me round a great tree trunk and made its escape.

Later on that morning, when in turns we sometimes fly fished from the shore, sometimes from the boat, casting out alongside the weed beds even higher up the lagoon, I got a six-pound rainbow and a four-pound rainbow in quick succession. Neither were spectacular fish, although they were both in fine end of season condition, and they were both distinctively liv-eried, with black star-shaped spots more reminiscent of a sea trout – albeit that this water was in no way connected with the sea and was indeed as far inland, and as distant from the sea, as it is possible to get in Tasmania. It was probably the silvery general impression of these rainbows that seemed reminiscent of sea-run steelhead such as I have seen in North America.

Alan caught and released a couple of four-poundish fish, but kept a fine hen rainbow of a shade under five pounds he took from the shallow weedy top water. By mid-afternoon there were signs that tonight's frost would be hard and come early. As if in a way of a signal the trout went deep and dis-interested; almost as if none were left in the lagoon. Before re-embarking in the boat for the journey across the lagoon back to the hut, I had a few last casts out across a ghostly cemetery of drowned trees. As I slowly recovered line from the final cast, even now ever-expectant for that adrenalin pumping first strong pull of a taking fish, I could see a swathe of mist out over the water, swirling like sea smoke, and there hurrying homewards between the drowned tree tops was a single platy-pus. Like us he was probably packing up for the night. I hoped he'd had as good a day as I had.

We fished next day until early afternoon; all without a touch, then reluctantly packed up the station wagon and head-ed back towards Hobart and the apples still ripening for the myriad soon-to-be Hajis along the desert road from Jeddah to Mecca.

There was a while to go yet; at least another week before loading the ship was completed. A few days later I accompa-nied Alan Henry while he was on a work inspection trip to a new hydro project at Gowrie Park, not far inland from

Devonport on the north coast. We stayed overnight at Deloraine, then returned to Hobart via Great Lake. The journey took us across moorland country, although the lake itself is surrounded by hills and alpine eucalypt forest.

The watershed has a great network of feeder streams, often so small and insignificant at first sight to seem little more than narrow ditches draining the moss and sparse alpine tussocks. They are often networked and intertwined in maze-like complexities; not merely tributaries to some greater stream. And they all provide unique spawning redds for brown trout. In several different places we stopped the car and walked over the mossy tussock. The ditches themselves are so narrow in places that crossing over them presents no difficulties.

But, as I was to see, most of them were full of spawning trout – all browns. Even in New Zealand I have never seen trout in such vast numbers, in such shallow, narrow waterways, so bent on their procreative imperatives that one might have stepped into the water and on to their backs and they would not have taken to instant flight. Indeed, in many more favoured places they were so densely packed, there was simply no place for them to go; so they stayed put and got on with the procreative procedures.

I have often watched such activities in New Zealand spawning streams, but often observed the intruding endeavours of a second male interloping fish, hurtling in to try and fertilise the ova deposited by the shuddering orgasmic hen fish ahead of the cock fish alongside her on the redd. Or even of a small, precocious male, dashing in from the wings in an attempt to do the deed. But here in the myriad spawning streams and ditches draining into Great Lake in Tasmania I saw little direct evidence of such precocious, interloping, sexual jealousies. It seemed more that with such a jam-packed density of writhing, spawning fish, there was either an exact one to one division of the sexes, or that they were all paired off to their complete satisfactions, or that the sheer numbers and density of their mass behaviour was such that one would not have noticed adulterous practices anyway: least of all the trout themselves.

The spawning trout took no notice of our presence whatsoever. Fortunately, for their sakes, Tasmania is a relatively sparsely populated and island State, and this spawning place was remote from the few real centres of population. Fortunate, too, that most Tasmanians who would be there at such a time are themselves dedicated fly fishermen and conservationists at heart – only too pleased to see the trout in their ritual dance ensuring their population increase for future angling seasons.

Even in New Zealand I have witnessed great marauding raids upon the totally pre-occupied activities of spawning trout, with sweep nets, pitchforks and shovels being used to get them out – and this by mostly indigenous people who think they have every right to do so: both moral, ethical right, and the right of ownership.

Never before, or since, have I ever seen trout in such numbers, massed up so spectacularly. It was so unreal, that it seemed unreal, and what was happening there right before my eyes took on the quality of a dream. But it was very real and all in deadly earnest.

The place itself seemed so unlikely. All around the countryside is often rock-strewn, particularly on the windward sides of small uprising knolls, prominent above the great stretches of tussock and moss interspersed by these ribbons of soaks, trickles, creeks, and larger streams connecting up with tarns and more distant lakes. Here and there, among the outcrops of rocks were patches of the ubiquitous Flame Bush, and even the occasional Snow Gum, struggling for survival with a tenuous foothold in the rocks, bent and twisted by the winds that often come in full southwesterly gales across the highland plateau, straight from the Roaring Forties of the Southern Ocean. Between the clumps of bushes were ankle-wrenching islands of button and snowgrass, and everywhere the pewter glint of ribbons of water, teeming with spawning trout, as far as the eye could see.

An interesting paradox in the ways of trout is now observable in the myriad lakes of the highlands of central Tasmania. Comment has been made of the maze of often inter-connecting creeks, gutters, natural drainage channels, streams and burns connecting and inter-connecting, linking up great lakes, small tarns, and innumerable rivers across this great watershed. Despite the earlier introduction of brown trout, and despite their continuing success as a species, the rainbow trout has outclassed the brown in the man-made fisheries management decisions to designate virtually all the larger waters as dedicated rainbow trout fisheries. And despite the fact that the brown trout still flourishes – mightily.

The paradox lies in the generally perceived nature of the two species. The rainbow is considered to be the eternal wanderer, ever eager to spread, migrate, go off to new places. The brown trout, contrarily, is thought to be the stay-at-home, resident, unwandering species. And in this context I do not mean whether either of the two species may have genetic or acquired sea-going tendencies where access to the sea is available to them, but rather the spread of either or both species through natural population increase in inter-connected freshwater systems.

In New Zealand waters connected to the sea, given half a chance the rainbows tend to move seawards, but in doing so are mostly gone forever, never to return. Unlike their steelhead cousins in the Pacific Northwest they seem not to obey any subsequent imperative to make the reverse spawning run into their natal or any other fresh water. Sea-run browns, on the other hand, seem mostly to stay close inshore and may return to fresh water either randomly, or specifically prior to spawning.

Yet in Tasmania the brown trout has spread throughout virtually every nook and cranny interconnected by ribbons of fresh water, colonising each new water in turn, until they exist everywhere. There is hardly a single salt water estuary where the tides comingle with outgoing fresh water that does not hold a good head of large, often huge, sea-run browns. Meanwhile, the Tasmanian acclimatised rainbow seems to have become a stay-at-home. Unless provided with suitable spawning grounds their numbers will need to be augmented by hatchery introductions. Their roles, it seems, have been reversed.

Great Lake is a most interesting impoundment of fresh water. Like most lakes in Tasmania it has suffered, or been improved, (depending on your point of view) by man's interference. In its natural state Great Lake was an extensive expanse of shallow water, fed by several feeder streams. Brown trout were first stocked in 1870, when 120 fingerlings were carried in on horseback in billy-cans. Then in 1910 there was an introduction of 5500 fingerling rainbow trout.

Both species thrived, establishing self-sustaining populations. Their progeny grew to great size. By the turn of the nineteenth century some of the brown trout were huge. A 25-pounder was caught in March 1897. Four years earlier a fisherman took 85 brown trout during April alone, from just under two to more than eighteen pounds. In 1904 another angler recorded a catch of 30 brown trout averaging nine pounds; among which were two fish of 18 pounds.

The lake was dominated by brown trout until the 1920s, when, for about twenty years, rainbow trout became the dominant species. From the early 1940s to the present day brown trout have once again dominated the fishery.

Interestingly, during the boom period for anglers at Great Lake, from the early 1920s to the late 1930s, when the rainbow trout thrived and became the dominant species, their predominance over brown trout in anglers' catches was reported to be 50 to 1, although the ratio in spawning runs in one of the most typical spawning streams was about 10 to 1. This, of course, may be due to the methods generally employed by anglers. As was found in New Zealand in the Taupo fishery, rainbows vastly outnumbered browns in anglers' catches, and for many years it was supposed that the population of browns was fast declining, and that they were probably on their way to extinction because of the more aggressive and gregarious habits of rainbows.

There was something in the ratios; but only something. The rainbows were simply easier to catch, and the brown trout harder. In Great Lake itself there were continuing swings in the trout populations. By the end of the post-war 1945-50 period the fishery had fallen into sad disrepute because of the poor condition and small size of the trout. The ratio of browns to rainbows had fallen to 1:1 in anglers' catches, but browns dominated the spawning runs by 10 to 1.

The pundits of the time gave all manner of reasons to account for the early success then dwindling fortunes of the trout fishery, but failed to identify the real culprit: man's intervention and interference. A major change occurred in 1922 with the construction of a dam at the outlet of the Shannon River. This added 25 feet to the depth of the lake. Even more importantly the Ouse River was diverted into Great Lake via the Liawenee Canal. When first completed the new channel provided six miles of uniform gravel substrate most suitable for spawning. By now, as a result of man's intervention, the main body of the lake was some fifteen miles in length and seven miles across. At this time it was possible to maintain the water level at a constant height, thus benefiting the regeneration of trout populations.

Several years of stable lake levels were followed by disastrous years of drastic manipulation of water level and draw-offs for hydro purposes: many ill-thoughtout and senseless. Throughout this period the new Liawenee Canal was progressively concreted, reducing the spawning area to the lower half-mile or so of the steeper, scoured, coarse substrate of limited spawning value. This situation persists to this day.

A recent observer has said that when the Great Lake fishery was at its best during the 1920s and 1930s, rainbow trout spawned in thousands on gravel areas around the lake margins, but that this behaviour depended on stable high water levels. When suddenly fluctuating water levels began to take their toll on the rainbow trout population, the brown trout numbers increased, until once again they predominated. The brown trout had established significant spawning areas in other tributary streams in Great Lake that remained accesssible despite the lowered water levels. It was said that once they became established in large numbers on the now limited spawning beds, the brown trout's earlier spawning time gave this species a significant advantage over the later spawning rainbows, and the era of rainbow dominance came to an end.

It was said that where both species co-exist on the spawning grounds, young brown trout are big enough to eat rainbow fry by the time the latter emerge. Furthermore, the late spawning of rainbows also results in the hazard of redds and nursery streams drying up before the fry have migrated downstream.

Interestingly, while this was happening in Tasmania, and such were the findings of those responsible for managing the fisheries, a somewhat different theory was gaining official credence across the Tasman Sea in New Zealand. There, in the Taupo fishery, where browns and rainbows had seemed to be in similar environmental conflict with each other, it was deemed that the later spawning rainbow trout significantly reduced future populations of brown trout by digging over and destroying their redds already awaiting the hatching of the earlier deposited fertilised brown trout ova.

The Tasmanian response was to embark upon a programme of removing what they considered to be "unthrifty" adult brown trout from the spawning beds in the Liawenee Canal, transfering them to other less well endowed waters. This was coupled with a massive programme of stocking with hatchery raised rainbow trout.

As a management policy it seemed to prove of dubious value. Designed to boost the proportion of rainbow trout in the anglers' catch it seemed to balance unequally against the

1983-84 official finding of an accurate count of spawning trout passing through the fish trap in Liawenee Canal revealed that brown trout still outnumbered rainbows by 18 to 1.

Robert Sloane has reported that following the most recent dam works completed in 1986 the height of the impoundment was increased six metres to 28 metres. Simultaneously most of the fallen and drowned timber has been removed from the lake itself, although trees extend to the full supply level of the eastern shores. Although brown trout still outnumber rainbow trout by 18 to 1 in their respective spawning runs, the ratio in anglers' bags is closer to 2 to 1. The water is still "managed" as a rainbow fishery.

Nowadays, the trout average two to four pounds, with individual fish to five pounds not uncommon. Rainbows tend to be better conditioned than many of the browns and account for the greater percentage of larger fish caught. Despite a phenomenal normal rise and fall of 21 metres for hydro purposes, and the consequent lack of stable margins, shallow weedbeds and fluctuations of depth of water over the important offshore trout feeding areas of muskgrass beds, it still seems to provide excellent fishing. Although, I for one, am glad that I first came to know it before such major engineering.

There was no such rise and fall during my first visits. The incredible spawning activities I saw that first day with Alan Henry must, of necessity, have ceased if low water levels occur as the spawning runs commence.

But on that first day by the myriad spawning streams around Great Lake it was no time or place for fishing, and we made our way back towards Hobart.

Meanwhile the loading of apples had slowed almost to a halt, and had I been a more worrying sort of mariner I suppose I would have been more overly concerned for the fortunes of my shipping company employers in London. But this was how things were done in those days (albeit that nowadays claims are made that revolutionary changes have been made:

46

that such business practices have been modernised, vastly improved, whereas all that has occurred has been relentless change, not necessarily for the better, and often much for the worse. If you wish to test my words then think of this next time you bite into an Australian or New Zealand apple, shipped half-way around the world, then remember how much better they used to be before shipping methods were revolutionised for the 'better.') My commercial masters in London were no more worried than were their local managers in Australia, or the Apple & Pear Board, or the waiting entrepreneurial desert sheiks who stood to make a financial killing out of the pilgrims once the apples got to Saudi Arabia, so why was I to care too much?

Reflect, too, that the apple consignment for Saudi Arabia, about which the ship's entire loading programme hung, consisted of less than one two-hundredth part of this one ship's total cargo of apples, let alone the other general cargo. It is not just in foreign places that things are done differently; we ourselves always do things far more differently than we choose to remember.

Instead, just three days later, I accepted another invitation to go fishing with Alan Henry. This time he took me to the eponymous Lagoon of Islands, a little way south and east of Great Lake. I knew it would be the last fishing day of that particular visit to Tasmania, when all such occasions seem to take on a special significance. Because of the shallow, weedy nature of the lake, and of the best fly-fishing it affords, Alan decided to trailer his boat from Hobart.

Once again the day was fine, with clouds racing by a fitful autumn sun, and a cold wind coming out of the southwest with a vengeance. As everywhere in this beautiful island State of Australia the journey was a delight, through old established and lush farm lands at first, before climbing up on to the first of the steppe-like ridges towards the Great Western Tiers.

The Lagoon of Islands is encircled by rolling hills of dry sclerophyll bushland. Its foreshores are mostly flat, grassy and open, and the lagoon – being almost circular in shape – seems at first sight to be a regular, almost featureless expanse of water, but small and knowable. Once embarked in the boat, however, with fly rods set up and ready, what Alan had told me about it on the way north became visibly apparent. Not only are the lake margins thick with weed and dense growths of rushes, but the main body of the lagoon is all but covered with prolific weedbeds and mats of rushes. Although the unique floating ti-tree islands were killed off when the level of the original lagoon was raised for hydro-electric purposes two years earlier, they are clearly visible across the lake surface.

To me there was something strange about it: the boat, quietly and gently penetrating between and through beds of reeds and rushes and the drowned ti-tree scrub. The water was shallow, and the strong wind and quite considerable chop on the water churned up the silt, so that long streaks of dull grey opacity took on the form of wind lanes in which one might expect trout feeding – but weren't, and were fishless places. We edged along in the boat. With fly rod in hand at the ready, I kept thinking of the seeming incongruity of the place.

It seemed for all the world as if we were navigating through a vast rice paddy – as if it was a laughable idea that the water held any trout whatsoever. A cast here and there, following the example of my mentor, produced nothing but an invariably weed-hung fly. There was something soothing in this penetration through the reeds and rushes.

Like most Tasmanian trout fisheries, Lagoon of Islands has had its ups and downs, its good years as well as bad. Although managed as a rainbow trout fishery it still holds a considerable self-sustaining stock of brown trout. At the time of which I write there were only restricted spawning sites for brown trout. Since then an important spawning stream has been created by diverting Ripple Creek into the lake. Rainbows always fared better. I had been advised to expect fish of between three and ten pounds, almost certainly rainbows this late in the season, but so far it seemed that one would spend more time in ridding one's fly of weed than in having full confidence that it was out there, in the water, unweeded and fishing as it should.

We drifted down through a channel close by a thick weedbed near the shore where one of the few belts of lakeside trees extended right down to the water's edge. Alan was casting towards the weedbeds, working his fly back towards the boat. He cast again, and his fly all but alighted on the thick, impenetrable mat of weed close by the shore. It plopped into the water and as he pulled the line hard to make direct contact with the fly his rod bent almost double as a fish tore off line and disappeared under the weed.

I could see his fly line cutting through the thick weed, throwing up a spray of water and piled up weed wherever it moved. And it wasn't altogether going straight, as say a wire cutter going through cheese, for the fly line would sometimes change its track under the buildup and pressure of the surface weed, and sometimes the hooked trout would similarly alter course – so that two sections of his fly line sometimes seemed to be moving in not the same direction.

Then came a lull in the proceedings when, without any disclosed knowledge of where the trout lay, or what it was doing, it was possible for him to get back some line on to the reel. As he did so and increasing strain came on the rod – not as a result of the trout's exertions, but simply due to the sheer dead weight of the intervening bunched up .weed, the fish came heading out from under the thick blanket of weed. The first thing either of us became aware of was a great leap out of the water not far out from the boat – while at the same time the weed encrusted fly line still embedded in the weedbed came out very much more slowly.

For awhile, until he had handlined the great bight of weed-held line from out of the inshore bed, the hooked trout lay tethered, as it were, about five or six yards out from the boat. I could see it clearly, tugging and rubbing against the intruding hold it felt against its freedom coming not from the boat, which the trout no doubt could clearly see, but in no way associated with its plight, but from inshore, from the very safety of the weedbed it had sought.

In my judgement, even conservatively, it was an exceedingly bright rainbow of about eight pounds, with only the faintest tinge of purple along its flanks. In that moment the trout had no association between us and the boat, and the discomfiture it felt tethering it to the weedbed.

With a final hand pull, the last of the entrapped bight of fly line came away. For a few moments there was no contact between fish and the weed bed, or between fisherman and fish, and in this brief span of time the trout visibly shot into action. It turned and streaked off down the lake, parallel to the weedbeds and shoreline, then moved out a little and went deeper and dogged.

Twice more it came away and ran this way and that, and after the second run Alan gained line on the fish as it came towards the boat. I was even readying the landing net, but the trout had other intentions. It ran back into the shoreline fringe of weed, but this time angled out obliquely some distance along the shore. Then it wrapped itself around a small protruding island of rushes. I even saw the fish coming out of the inshore channel around it, while Alan's fly line was still going around the other side, in the opposite direction. The trout kept going to safety. Alan's fly line went slack, and the episode was done, as he reeled in with his fly and all his leader tippet gone. We tucked the boat into the lee behind a sheltering belt of rushes and ate our sandwiches and drank welcome mugs of hot coffee. An hour later, back fishing in this rice-paddy- like maze of weedbeds, reeds and rushes, and drowned ti-tree, I cast my fly almost up to the weed, pitching it into a foaming, white scummy aggregate of wind-blown, wind- collected debris. I was sure the fly had picked up a twig or broken off reed blade because the fly line seemed to hang on the water with none of the subtle dynamics one might have reasonably expected from it sinking uninterruptedly through the surface layers of water. Then, for a moment, I thought I was hooked into a more solid, unmoving snag. When the snag exploded and I was fast into a leaping rainbow that first streaked across the lake, the fly line ssoon collecting its cargo of weed in its curving parabolic path, but only enough of it to hinder the fish, rather than aid its escape. The encroaching weed came away from my fly line as soon as the trout changed direction, but the initial pull against the fish had taken its toll, for it allowed itself to be reeled in and led towards the boat like a dog on a lead. With no more than a single half-hearted run at the sight of the net it came in on the next shortening and slipped over the landing net rim into the enfolding entrapment of the mesh. While I hate any articial prolongment of the so-called "playing" of a fish, and feel they should be netted or beached or released with some alacrity, I was still surprised that this particular rainbow jack came in with relatively little opposition. It was a well-conditioned and deep-bodied, thick in the shoulder rainbow in as good a state of being as any I'd seen that season. That was the end of our fishing that day at the Lagoon of Islands. The wind was blowing hard and we had great difficulty in making it back through the weedy shallows, and getting the boat on to its trailer. But it had been a good fishing day, and I knew it would be the last trout fishing expedition of that voyage.

It was back to Hobart. We called at Wentworth House at Bothwell, the home of Alan's parents-in-law, on the return journey, where we enjoyed a splendid supper. The house was very beautiful; a lovely example of early colonial architecture; a haven of elegance and fine living, not hours away from the wildness of the central highlands we had known that day.

I was well content to reach Hobart, make my farewells, go onboard my ship with fly rods stowed away, and ready for sailing soon afterwards towards those deserts of Saudi Arabia with a part-cargo of sweet and juicy apples from the blessed land of Tasmania.

OUT IN THE BACK COUNTRY

A river is never silent. Even its
deepest pools thrive with dark
or dreamy utterance. They shelter
more than we can say we know.

Brian Turner

Over the years in Taupo Bill and Nick and I fell into the observance of two regular rituals in our angling almanac. We celebrated Opening Day each first day of October really as a celebration of the event of going fishing on the first day of a new season. Good white wine, stream-cooled on the inevitably cold first day out, and more special picnic food than usual was the order of the day. Such a ritual came about that Bill even suggested we should all wear ties on that auspicious, longed for day, because Halford and Skues would be watching us from their celestial stream banks and   would not approve of our usual casualness of dress – albeit that we were quite alone in some of the wildest loneliest high country in New Zealand.   But over the years another event became rit- ualized in our fishing year. Once, almost always in early December, by which time the weather would have warmed up, but still not be the heat of midsummer, we would go off on a longer fishing trip to some even wilder, less accessible place, and camp.

This tale is of one such trip that took us to the very mountainous inner heart of the North Island of New Zealand, almost as unapproachable in its wild and mountain fastness as the secret regions of Tibet. By the time of this my first visit it was approachable by a road of sorts – a track really, hewn and slashed out of the dense native bush, across deep steep-crin-kled valleys squashed out from the land, as if in some primor-dial creation the sort of country the rest of the world is made up of had been squeezed in from all sides, tightly, so that mountain, valley and river systems that ought properly have extended over thousands of square miles had been unceremo-niously bundled into just a few hundred.

Anyone who has flown over this part of New Zealand can perhaps imagine what it must be like down there on the ground; otherwise comparisons can do it no justice. Wild though it is, grandeur there is none. For a start, everything is on top of everything else, so that there are no vistas; nothing that sweeps the eye to distant peaks and places: it is all bunched up – at least until one gets in to where we were going.

Long before our visit much of the land hereabouts was in private hands, belonging to a big forestry company, with just one dirt road in – not even improved enough for the eventual harvesting task of getting out the yet to be felled great forests still growing. But the preparations for forestry in such a place and on such a scale are not beautiful to behold. The old native bush of age-old beech, rimu, and pongas, had been savagely and unbeautifully cleared, and despite ten years or more of reforestation and regeneration the steep hills and valleys were scarred and savaged.

In the topmost, least accessible places the more gentle native bush was reasserting itself, but it, too, was scarred and misshapen, while below the exotic but less lovely pine forests shot skywards, disciplined, marshalled, slender and tall – all destined to grow fast in the pumice soil, to be turned into woodchip and toilet rolls in Japan at some later date. This was their destiny. Only the sheer angularity and steepness of the landscape saved it from being ugly. There was pumice dust everywhere. Fortunately, we did not see another car or a logging truck on the way in, so that the dust was all of our own making and behind us, like a great writhing grey billowing snake up and down the steep terrain from which we had emerged.

It was private land and the road, such as it was, belonged to the same corporate owner. Thanks to Nick we had obtained rarely given permission to go in and camp at our chosen destination. It was hard to tell whether it was all a sort of ghost place of failed and forgotten enterprises, or a place, yet to be born. According to the survey map we passed by several places with names with nothing recognisable to mark them as specific places. We saw nothing, for they were empty of any sign of human visitation, let alone habitation, apart from the winding, tortuous dirt road that seemed to go on and on forever. They were simply names on a map waiting for something to happen, but such parts of New Zealand have a habit of swallowing up all visible signs of man's handiwork, as well as of his naming of them, as if they had never been.

There were Pakeha placenames, given no doubt by some early prospecting white settlers in the early days of the colony. And they were all totally inappropriate of the actual places as if those who gave them names were seeing what the wanted to be seeing, rather than the wilder alien reality of what they were. In such manner we went through and passed by Willowflat – as inappropriately named a place as any I have ever passed by. Closer to our remote destination the NZ Lands & Survey map told us we were travelling along Pie Cart Road, and I couldn't help wondering what sort of wag so named it: had he been hungry and dreaming of that one-time great New Zealand national institution, the town and city pie cart, or was it a mirage dreamed up out of loneliness.

Most of the placenames were Maori because, even long before Captain Cook's first arrival, the Maori tribes travelled lightly through such country and like the Aboriginals of central Australia they sang the land into existence, giving every place a special name, endowing special places with spiritual significance, while others were named descriptively, so that names were like maps, enabling those who came after them to follow the same tracks and "know" the place. And in the fastness there, even the leader of one of the great uprisings of the Maori against the white settlers was duly celebrated where at the summit of a conglomeration of tight-packed mountain peaks the map declared the place to be Te Kooti's Lookout. And in there lay our destination.

We diverted a little to look in at the ruins of the Te Hoe Logging Camp, then back south again, along an even worse dirt road, but with occasional tantalising glimpses of the Te Hoe River far below us, like a shining silver ribbon threaded through the dappling light of tens of thousands of pines. But these signs and sightings of the river were almost vertically downwards, down precipitous slopes. It was rough, hard country. At last, after what seemed like a never-ending journey to nowhere, and a steep descent down into a wider – but much wider – valley, we came to an old wooden bridge across a creek out of the Te Hoe Stream itself, so solid in the great hewn blocks of native timber from which it had been constructed that it seemed as if it had been there since the beginning of time. We stopped the station wagon and tested the bridge, but for safety's sake, as well as in case of a sudden flash flood cutting us off had we crossed, we decided to carry our packs and tents and fishing gear the last half mile or so to our camping place.

Hereabouts was the first bit of more or less flat land we had seen since coming in off the Napier-Wairoa road early that morning. There was a flattish stretch of tussock leading down to a stream that spread out over a broad shallows before virtually disappearing again through a small cleft between two great overhanging boulders, and tumbling down beyond in a series of steep falls and stony pools before becoming quite inaccessible by foot. Upstream at the head of the gentle pool there was a run of fast white broken water, then a steep climb

55

up over a series of falls and pools into a thick canopy of native bush.

Here we were at the confluence of two mountain streams; the Te Hoe, the larger of the two, and the Hautapu River. And there, close by a broad and shallow pool we set up our tents and made camp.

A hurried supper of easily prepared food gave us time to set up our fly rods and have a couple of hours fishing the Te Hoe before dark. It was lovely fishing. Going up through that first fast white water with a Hare & Copper nymph chucked up ahead of me, searching out the dark edges of the far side, I hooked a good rainbow on the third or fourth cast, but it leapt to a well-deserved freedom right up in the foaming head of the pool, under a huge overhanging boulder, and sped away to safety.

I climbed from pool to pool, upwards into the steeply ter-raced stream, here and there interspersed with deep, glidey, magic looking pools, hooking and releasing a small rainbow of about two pounds along the way. But such was the nature of the stream I wanted to be pressing on, for up under the canopy of native bush there would be shade and shelter and perhaps more expansive pools and riffles, and more of the mystery I suppose I best enjoy to accompany my fishing. There was no time for it that night, so we returned to camp, made billy tea, drank a whisky together by the side of our fire, then crept into our sleeping bags even as the last of twilight darkened out of the sky. It was a good feeling.

Next day there had to be the ritual breakfast of eggs and bacon and sausages before setting off individually. Nick chose the Hautapu Stream. Bill and I set off further upstream in the Te Hoe, fishing up through some small pools on the way. After an hour or so we split up: he taking a diversion to reach the stream again about a mile up the steep valley; while I fished up through the bigger series of deep pools and runs, each interspersed by steep waterfalls and sunlit shallows.

It was lovely fishing: blissful just to be there. Some of the pools were bush girt, while others were quite open to the sky with no cover but for huge round weather-worn boulders. These last were generally very deep pools. The water clarity was startling and confusing, with depths going down to twenty or more feet and every stone and boulder and patch of glistening sand on the bottom standing out as if covered by no more than a few feet of water. Because of the lie of the stream and my upstream approach, combined with the morning sun, it was still not easy to discern the trout lying deep in the pools. I tended to see mere shimmers of movement, revealing a different pattern than that of the water and dappling light over the boulders and stones, and then I saw where a great trout had been, rather than where it was. There were always great boulders against the stronger edge of the pool where the water ran fastest, but on the other side there was usually a steep sandy beach where a hundred years of back eddies had deposited the fine dark sand.

But these inviting little beaches of sand were treacherous. To start with they were steep-sided, and softly steep-sided, and led straight off into water twenty or more feet deep. Even a boot advanced cautiously a few inches out into the mere wetness seemed like a quicksand, so I soon learned to rely more upon the less easy to negotiate boulders.

New Zealand streams such as these are paradoxical in matters concerning their trout populations. They appear to be – and are – only sparsely endowed with fly and other insect life, especially in such deep pools. Yet such streams – and such pools in particular – tend to hold relatively small populations of relatively large trout – especially if they are rainbows. Remoteness and the fastness of the place itself is no exception, but such trout are invariably most difficult to catch and incredibly line and leader shy. A single cast alighting ahead of them is usually enough to send them all into a panic; not least that the ensuing commotion of perhaps half a dozen big, but varying size trout, will entirely displace their previous rigid territorial pecking order, and it may take half-an-hour before they all jostle around and resume their rightful and jealously guarded sequential positions.

One of the humiliating aspects of such pools in such places is in their contradictoriness. The questing fly fisherman who has got to such a place with so much effort is quite convinced that these trout he sees have grown as big as they are – seven, eight, nine, ten pounds or more – without having ever seen a humanbeing, let alone an angler. So it seems as if they would be easy to catch. But show them the shadow of a fly line, or a six foot length of the finest leader tippet on the water, and they go into s frenzy, charging around their home pool like maniacal trout.

As for nymph fishing there is the not inconsiderable problem – nay, the impossibility – of getting even the heaviest weighted nymph down deep enough in the water before it is swept into the usually fishless tail of the pool. In almost all such attempts the deep-lying trout never even see the angler's artificial nymphs.

Indeed, the best hope of success, and by far the most exciting, is to float a big dry fly over them. Paradoxically, they won't rise to a nymph passing fifteen feet above their heads, but will often rise with gusto to a dry fly at twenty. What is more they will often chase such a floating fly down the pool if they see it only after it has passed by. The trouble is in getting the dry fly hard enough into the neck of the pool to ensure it has the maximum float directly above the head of the phalanx of deep-lying trout, but still contrive the (uually) short cast to be delivered in such a fashion that no drag ensues, but that no fly line on the water gives rise to panic the trout.

Indeed, if all goes well, and the float of the fly is enticing enough, the dominant fish at the head of the pool will be seen to be rising almost aldermanically, as if the observed morsel was his by right. Only when he sees another lesser fish lying astern of the prime feeding position, but coming up more positively, will he react. In such a combination of circumstances (and I must confess to have experienced the delight only on

58

half a dozen occasions) the senior trout will shoot to the surface like a Polaris rocket being fired, engulfing the fly and taking it down in one continuous splashy, heady movement. Giddily exciting stuff for the angler on the bank, but tempered by the hard facts that the pool will be deep (and full of snags); and small (and once the hooked trout decides to vacate it, either upstream or down, that is invariably that); and in order to fool the trout into taking the fly in the first place the leader needs to be so gossamer fine that the fish will still have advantage on his side (and almost always has). But, while it lasts, what bliss!

On that first exploratory clamber up the upper reaches of the Te Hoe Stream there were no trophy trout caught – at least not to my rod. In all I lost three trout of unverified size, and caught and released three more; the best about 5 pounds – all on a Hare & Copper nymph. All the fish caught were rainbows; not a single brown trout did I sight that day.

It was delightful fishing: a sort of fly-fishing in miniature, because the nature of the terrain changed so much in every hundred yards or so of relatively easy going, that each new pool and run and riffle was like fishing an entirely new place. In the dappled, gladey runs, usually surrounding the longer, shallower pools, there were still stands of old pongas shading the multitude of ferns, with old and crazily gnarled relics of beech trees leaned and tottered over the water. It was fishing in an ancient, primitive landscape.

At one point, just when I thought I was all alone in the world, and was treading along a mountain stream bank where perhaps no man had walked for many years, I was brought back to harsher realities. I had climbed up and over a series of fast, stony runs, each one rising a yard or two but creating the illusion that the downstream lip of what I took to be a wide pool opening back from the skyline ahead of me was steeper than it actually was; and hence more inviting to move towards it.

Then, suddenly, I was there. A crystal clear pool lay in

front of me; perhaps no more than twenty feet long, and rather less in width. A great tumble of large boulders guarded the upstream limit of the pool, and the water came into it through a deep gulley, fast and strong. Directly below this head of the pool there broadened out a sheet of scintillating deep water. A single penny lying on the bottom would have been clearly visible. What lay more strikingly than a penny on the bed of the pool was a huge boulder, smooth and almost perfectly rounded, itself perhaps ten feet tall, but still at least that depth beneath the limpid surface water that gurgled expansively as it spread out in the pool from the confines of the narrow cleft above. It was perhaps no more than the angle and height of the sun at that particular time, but never before, or since, have I seen a deep pool of such startling clarity and perfection.

Indeed, so intense and intent was my gaze into its depths, searching for the tell-tale shimmer of a trout, that I failed at first to notice that on the narrow strip of sandy beach encircling the far, stiller side of the pool were the clear indentations of several bootprints.

Cautiously, I edged my way around to them. Footsteps in the sand they were indeed, and recent at that by their appearance. The forest manager had told us, I had thought, that no one had been in or fished this stream for two years, yet these footprints could not have been more than a few weeks old at the most.

I had come up over the downstream cascade all set to cast, wary in case it would prove to be one of those one- chance, one-cast pools. Long before first sighting the alien footprints reminding me I was not alone in the world, I had the artificial nymph out of the keeper, held in my left hand, with the leader outside the rod tip and my rod all primed for a quick cast if I sighted a trout, as I felt sure I would.

The footprints did put me off a bit, and take me higher up the pool than I would have gone, so when I began casting up towards the head of the pool it was little more than a response to a reflex action – certainly not to a sighted fish, although out of the peripheral edge of my vision I did think I had possibly seen the dappled blink of shadow of a deep-lying trout. It was still there several casts later, but deep beyond the reach of my fly, so I put on a more heavily weighted caddis imitation and chucked it up on to the nearside rock at the head of the pool, so that it slid off and sank into the deep water.

I remember watching it go down, the dressing glistening in its tumbling descent, as if by entrapped air bubbles in the dubbing. Then as I sought to gather in line to make proper positive contact with the fly there was a sudden tug in my hand; not the rug-tug-tug of a good trout, but as if I had hooked into something elastic. I had.

Once I had regained all the slack line it was obvious that the bend of the rod tip, and the tug in my fingers was being imparted only by my own actions. No living thrumming thing was on the other end. I moved sideways on to the sandy beach, lay down my rod, reel inside my hat, and handlined the few yards of fly line still outside the rod tip. It took some pulling in, but came all the same, albeit getting tighter and springier with every foot regained. Then it would yield no more, but still like a coiled spring.

By moving upstream along the side of the pool and getting abreast of the obstruction, I was able to recover more line. Then something flashed brightly in the sunlight as my leader came into view, until I saw that my four-pound leader tippet and caddis imitation were hooked around a very stout bight of nylon monofilament curving away downwards into the depths of the pool. Knowing that the fine leader tippet would not stand much more of a strain, I rummaged around in my pack until I found the stoutest trout lure hook in my boxes, then tied it to some 20-pound nylon I had for leader butts and rigged this through my fly rod tip so that a small loop just above the new fly hook would slide down my snagged fly line, then over the stretched out leader and hopefully hook over the bight of the underwater nylon snag.

The first few attempts were unsuccessful, but just as I was

about to leave it and simply break off, losing no more than my fly and leader, but leaving the underwater snag as an unknown hazard in the pool, the substituted fly hook slid over the offending nylon and pulled tight. But even with the stronger nylon to heave on I could only bring the underwater bight of nylon within hands reach, and no further. One end was plainly snagged around the huge boulder at the bottom of the pool. The other end of the bight disappeared into a fissure between a group of smaller underwater boulders more towards my side of the pool. No amount of pulling would shift it, so I resolved to be satisfied with cutting the offending nylon. When I got in as much as possible it was plain to see it was a strong sea line, probably of fifty-pounds or more test. My fly scissors could hardly cut through it, but did, and I watched the cut ends sink down into the depths, as my nymph and leader came back to me.

In cutting this great bight of sea line I must have released the tension on one underwater end of it, and with a sudden flash of white out rolled from the fissure between the smaller boulders a plastic handcaster used by heave-ho sea fishermen. Except that this was at the very inland heart of New Zealand, about as far away from the sea as it is possible to get anywhere in those islands, and a place we had been told not even a bona fide fly fisherman had visited for at least two entire seasons.

Disappointed only to have cut the underwater snag and offending hazard, rather than have removed it altogether, I sat down nearby to take stock of the situation before moving on upstream, for there was no point in further fishing where I was. I sat down on a convenient stone, wondering who and when and with what purpose men with a deep-sea line had been fishing this remote mountain stream. Then I noticed some horse flies hovering nearby – and more of a congregation of them than might be expected. As I moved towards them I saw a flatter stone on which lay strips of meat, cut as bait, each about the size of a mouse, but all not quite so dessicated that I could tell they had not been there long – no more than a day or two at most.

The outcome of yet another digression in this tale was that on our way out, several days later, we called in to the forest caretaker's house to tell him we were out of his territory and on our way. I told him about the sea-caster and fifty-pound nylon and cut bait. He looked puzzled at first, as if he didn't believe me, then said, almost casually, "Oh, yes!. I know! A couple of months back we had a gang of Maori workers in, thinning out a section of trees. They camped for a few days. Probably set a night line for eels. You know how Maoris love eels!"

Despite that explanation, I still think the line had been set to catch big trout, not eels; and that the cut bait had not been lying on that rock for a couple of months. More puzzling still is that – albeit by day – the same trout that shies away from my three-pound leader tippet would surely not succumb to a lump of mutton attached to the hooked end of a 50-pound nylon sea line?

On that first day I carried on exploring and fishing until it was time to head back to the place far downstream where I had arranged to meet up with Bill. The going was easier and faster on the return.

By the time we got back to our camp I was pleasantly tired and not too uncomfortably made aware of calf and thigh muscles not used so much for several months. But it was a good feeling, and had been a good day.

And so was spent the remaining days we had there. Next day I fished the Hautapu; so different in character and style that they might have been streams a thousand miles apart, and not close tributary to each other. Five rainbows caught and released – the best again about 5 pounds – and two fish lost, the best of which may have been six or seven, that made its escape in some fast rapids where I had not the least chance of following it, or hope of stopping its departure.

Fortunately, the weather held until the afternoon we drove out. We hardly cleared Pie Cart Road before the heavens opened and the deluge started. In all likelihood, had we been still at our camp, the tents would have been washed away. Even as we descended towards the sealed highway and the road back home towards Taupo, great sheets of lightning ripped apart the ugly black storm-filled sky. The rain did not ease until we had crossed the mountainous divide between the Hawkes Bay coastal plain and Taupo. As we came over the hill an unseen shaft of burnished sunlight shone through the storm clouds massing over Acacia Bay and the lake suddenly sparkled in a shimmering golden glow.

Acacia Bay was home, hot baths, a very cold dry martini, a relaxed, unhurried evening meal, and a soft bed. However welcome such comforts were, there was a part of me still up there, clambering upstream along the fabulous Te Hoe Stream.

❊ ❊ ❊ ❊ ❊

As it happened, I never went back there, nor do I think that either Bill or Nick have re-visited the place. We always tried to vary the place of this annual camping/fishing ritual, but since then I have moved away and no longer share in it, except vicariously. This annual ritual continues with just Bill and Nick. Even as I write this I have had separate letters from them both, telling me of this year's expedition. They write in a sort of shorthand, which makes each of their letters well worth quoting verbatim, in a Rashomon-like way, because although they each tell of the same events they recount them almost as if I, too, was meant to be with them, as if we were all there together, sitting around a campfire, drinking whisky from tin mugs before climbing into our sleeping bags against the fast cooling shades of night – before another day's fishing.

The place they went to this year would only be perhaps thirty or forty miles as the crow flies from the Te Hoe of my present story, but even crows would find the journey hard going and cloud piercing, for the country in between is mountain wilderness; successions of steep river valleys and twisted soaring hills, dense native bush and forest; country rugged in the extreme.

This time, on this particular journey they flew in by chartered helicopter to one of New Zealand's most fabled wilderness trophy trout rivers. Here are their respective stories, just as they wrote them for me.

First, Bill's:

We had good weather for the trip to the Ngaruroro, flew from Poronui to the hut at the Gold Creek confluence, dropped off our gear then went downriver in the helicopter and fished back halfway to the hut, then climbed up a 200 foot bluff and tramped and scrambled back over the tussock. River gin clear, light coloured rocky to pebble bottom, easy wading and access never a problem making progress along at least one bank, pools down to 20 feet deep or more and fish four pounds to 10 pounds – possibly up to 15 pounds. They are constantly on the move, rarely occupy a specific feeding position; the "smaller" fish always appear to be jockeying for a better feeding station, challenging (if not seriously) the pecking order. The bigger fish then sees them off – they often mill around after the fly line is laid on the water, spot it, and —-! Didn't see a great deal of insect life – *Coloburiscus* hatching on the Wednesday, a few *Nesameletus* also. Nick landed one each day and pricked or lost a few. I pricked and lost one, took a lot of photographs, but made the mistake of leaving one camera behind, with the lens best suited to landscapes, and took in the 'micro' lens – not a good idea. There seemed to be small dark caddis coming off on Saturday, suspect caddis might form a substantial part of their diet. Little or no bush, one small patch a couple of hundred yards from the hut. Most of the bush could be seen on the tops or in the distance.

I spotted fish from a rocky outcrop perhaps 150 feet up, and Nick says 300 or 400 yards away. He might be right in his estimate of distance, but I was peeved to find next day that these fish were around 10 pounds, and that takes the edge off my optical feat. We discussed fishing with a "dry mouse," but in view of the size of the fish perhaps a "drowned rat" on a hi-density line might be more appropriate. A Tegel chicken might have been more appropriate still – with feathers, of course, but we considered that a hook in proportion with the "fly" might be illegal!

The hut had a shower, hot and cold water, and a flush loo – not a real man's hut, but very comfortable by comparison. Bought a tramper's mat from Outdoor Living – asked Tony Turner if he had a thicker one, and he said "real men" sleep on thin ones, so I asked him for six!

Nick wrote of it thus:

. . . . helicoptering in to the Ngaruroro river where we stayed in a hut at the junction of Gold Creek and Ngaruroro, some hour's walk downstream from the Boyd Hut. This is the trip we had talked about for a couple of years, but finally managed it – for five days. The first day was probably the best. The helicopter, having unloaded our gear then flew downstream and dropped us just above the gorge – well not actually dropped us – so we could fish upstream. The day was fairly sunny and the river amazingly clear – you could see right to the bottom of some pools up to 20 feet deep – these deep pools contained three to four fish – all rainbows – averaging 10 pounds, with the biggest fish perhaps 14-15 pounds.

However, with the water so clear it was not really possible to catch these big fish legally – perhaps a large dry fly at night – something like a whole chicken on a 5/O hook – other than removing the feathers and tying them on a hook – or a large deer-hair mouse. In fact I wondered if these fish did fatten up on mice – the rainbows were all in tremendous condition and yet we found little fly life in the river. Perhaps the mice lined up at night to play "dare" and see who could swim across to the other side before being eaten. As an example of the condition of these fish, on the last day I caught one on a small nymph – tied incidentally with fur from our tabby cat Chrissie and named – of course – the Chrissie nymph. The fish looked to be about three pounds when seen, but on landing, after a vigorous fight, it proved to be over five pounds. it was a short, deep fish in better condition than any trout from Lake Taupo and would be the equal of the best Otamangakau fish, deep bellied and heavy shouldered.

On that first day I hooked nine fish – the first seven all on a sparsely-hackled and sparsely-winged Royal Wulff #12, which I tied on some expensive but inferior barbless Partridge hooks. Of the first seven fish I broke off one while using three-pound nylon – then hooked it again, most surprisingly, a few minutes later using an identical fly – and was quietly congratulating myself not only for hooking one of these very spooky fish twice, but also because I could retrieve my other fly – when the hook came away. One other fish – a rainbow of about nine pounds – got off by boring upstream and wrapping the line round a rock – the other five fish came off after being hooked for about 10 to 20 seconds, and with the rest the hooks opened up one after another. Hence my comment about the inferior Partridge hooks. By the time I had hooked the seventh fish I had got past the frustrated stage to the mildly amused stage, but the seventh fish stayed on and was landed, a reasonable rainbow of about seven pounds.

The trek back to the hut was fairly tough along steeply sloping tussock hills, up and down steep gorges. Sitting by the hut in the evening I noticed some rises at the head of the pool downstream. I first tried a #14 Partridge & Orange as a drowned dun and hooked a fish briefly. Another fish was rising further up the pool and it took a spent hair-wing deer-hair fly. Again a very heavy fish, I could not stop it running upstream around some rocks.

So nine fish hooked, one landed. But I was very happy – the rising of the fish is the most exciting moment, whilst I am beginning to cringe at the fear and pain involved for the fish being played; hence I was happy to see the fish get away, though to land and see the size of the largest fish would have been interesting – particularly in view of my last day's three pounder that turned out to be over 5 pounds.

That first night was cold, the water froze in the hand basin and in the supply pipe, but the sun on the frost-covered tussock was a beautiful sight.

On the way downstream I had a graphic account of the water clarity and Bill's extraordinary eyesight when – way above one long pool – Bill spotted two fish at the tail of the pool, when they must have been 600 to 800 yards away. Eventually, after much prodding, I also saw the fish.

By mid-morning the weather changed – colder and cloudy with some rain at times – as it was for the next two days. The fish went deeper and were harder to tempt, I caught one on the second day on a dry fly – about five pounds. Bill hooked one on a nymph on the third day. Much time was taken up in exploring and photographing.

There was one amusing incident on the third day: we were sitting by a cliff eating lunch by one of the deep pools which held three very large and one small, about six pound fish. The six-pounder was chased back down to the tail of the pool by a larger fish of some 10 pounds plus, which meant that the larger fish was somewhat more accessible in water 10 to 12 feet deep rather than the head of the pool at 20 to 25 feet deep. As it came back up the pool I cast a nymph well ahead of it, let it sink, then twitched the nymph as the fish came by. It rose slowly in the water, coming straight towards us, opened its mouth and took the nymph.   But being a wise old fish it realised straight away and in an instant, too fast to set the hook, it ejected the fly and with a most surprised look on its face swam slowly away.

Bill and I have had a few other fishing days so far this sea-son – one each to Mohaka, Waipunga and Wanganui have produced few fish but have been enjoyable nonetheless for the photography and general banter. I have also had a trip down through Poronui to the upper Mohaka/Kaipo confluence on my mountain bike – it was on my birthday – a lovely day again and three nice fish – again all on a Royal Wulff.

* * * * *

Such was Nick's letter. No fish killed, and few, in terms of numbers, caught, and those that were all carefully released. For a contemporary English fly fisherman, whose territories were the small well-manicured stillwater trout fisheries with car park almost adjoining the water's edge, such fishing days might seem disastrous – and disastrously unproductive. That famed Wittgenstein of English trout fishing would no doubt remain silent about it – pondering, instead, on the piscatorial and literary wisdom and symbolism of the letter K.

But I, for one, know which fishing I would rather share.

THE GREAT SEA-RUN BROWN TROUT OF WAITUNA LAGOON

Dr Gunther, however, in his account of those for-warded to him, says (see *Field* newspaper, 9th January, 1892): "The specimens are most assuredly not salmon (*S. salar*); neither are they brown trout (*S. fario*). They are a kind of sea trout (*S. trutta*), looking extremely like the Irish white trout. But the different kinds of migratory sea trout are so closely allied to each other that it is almost a matter of impossibility to give an opinion on artificially-reared fish or their offspring."

Now, the extraordinary peculiarity of this opinion is that Dr Gunther says these fish were certainly not salmon (*S. salar*) nor *S. fario*, these being the only two kinds of fish that have ever been put in the river (the Selwyn River), while he calls them a kind of sea trout (*S. trutta*), which have never been placed either in this river or in any other within scores of miles of it. In other words, he says they were certainly neither of the kinds of fish that were placed in the river in thousands, but another kind of fish that has never been put there at all. But, what-ever they are, there are large numbers of salmonidae in the Aparima (Southland) Estuary from 1lb to 12lb in weight, and Mr A. N. Campbell,

the curator of the Southland society, informs me
that he has often seen them caught in the same net
at different times with red-cod (*Lotella bacchus*),
barracouta (*Thyrsites atun*), dogfish, elephant-fish,
mullet, flounders, &c., a plain proof that they can
live and thrive with these voracious fishes as soon as
they have attained a certain size.
W.H.Spackman, *Trout in New Zealand*, 1898
(New Zealand's first fishing book)

Brown trout taken from Dorsetshire to New
Zealand quickly acquired a migratory habit and
became large silvery fish, inhabiting the sea for the
most part, and ascending rivers to spawn.
W.L.Calderwood, *The Life of the Salmon*, 1907

The fish-shops of Dunedin I found remarkably
well supplied, and every morning my first walk
would be to see what the sea had sent up from Port
Chalmers to the marble slabs during the night.
There were generally fine salmon trout in the town
sub rosa, and it was no secret that the fishermen in
the tidal waters were in the habit of surreptitiously
catching fine specimens of that strictly preserved
fish.
William Senior, *Travel and Trout in the Antipodes*,
1880

For most readers unfamiliar with the actual place – and it is
an actual place – the very sound of the words Waituna
Lagoon may conjure up a vision of a gently sea-lapped South
Seas island lagoon; Gauguinesque wahines lying seductively
on palm-fringed coral strands of fine, hot sands, with waving
coconut palms dappling the tropic sun. Indeed, as all
Polynesian languages have common roots and hardly differ

71

from each other across the vast Pacific Ocean, and especially because the Polynesians were consistent in the manner in which they gave names to places, the chances are that there are many Waituna Lagoons spread across the South Pacific. The name means, literally, 'waters of eel' – 'eel water'. But the place I write of lies at the far southern tip of the South Island of New Zealand, with nothing but tiny Stewart Island between its storm-tossed shingle beaches and the icebound wastes of Antarctica. There is nothing tropical or balmy about the Waituna Lagoon of my story.

For most anglers New Zealand conjures up a vision of the justly famed rainbow trout waters of Lake Taupo and the Tongariro River, but few realise that splendid brown trout fishing exists in abundance in the South Island. Here there are streams meandering gently through water meadows; big and brawling snow-melt, fast-flowing mountain rivers; ribbon rivers; a vast proliferation of lakes – just about every condition and habitat the trout fisherman, and the trout, could desire.

At the far southern tip of the South Island, yet only twenty-three miles from Invercargill, the main city of the province of Southland, lies Waituna Lagoon. It is the home of a race of wild brown trout such as men dream of; almost legendary even in such a paradise of trout as New Zealand, but little known. Yet it is one of those places just a bit further on along a back road to nowhere than most anglers are prepared to go, and relatively few – even among New Zealanders – know of its existence.

Separated from the thundering surf of the ocean beach by a narrow spit of steeply shelving shingle, the lagoon itself is an incongruity of nature. Almost midway between the meandering estuaries of the Oreti and Mataura Rivers the coastline curves gently into Toetoes Bay. The beach is fine shingle pounded incessantly by the surf of the endless succession of Southern Ocean storms, sweeping across the Roaring Forties, uninterrupted from here to Antarctica.

Like a tenuous finger this shingle spit uncomfortably confronts the surf. In places it is less than fifty yards wide: the Southern Ocean on one side; on the other, the brackish, but often purely fresh water lagoon which drains the small spawning streams: the Waituna Stream itself, and another, Moffat Creek at the far eastern arm. Incongruous in its configuration it gives rise to incongruous circumstances. I have fly fished the lagoon proper for trout while, not fifty yards away another angler was surfcasting the ocean for blue cod.

Storm seas throw up the debris of the ocean in a confusing manner so that while one is fishing for trout in peat-stained water, the ground underfoot is often strewn with sponges and the empty egg cases of skate and rays..

Fed by the three ideal spawning creeks already mentioned, the enclosed lagoon stretches seven miles in an east-west direction parallel to the sea and averages about a mile in width. Four miles from the last road access at the eastern end, the enclosing shingle spit is sometimes breached by storms and strong tides in a deep and steep outlet gorged out of the shingle. Here in some years, particularly after winter storms and equinoctial gales sweeping in from the south, the outlet becomes blocked. Another storm might open it again and alter the configuration of the tidal channel.

While the shingle is breached, at the outlet proper at low tide the sea is a hundred yards away, the breakers folding and thundering on to the outside beach with a vicious undertow. Inside, meanwhile, the water of the lagoon are fresh and now almost peat-stained, while in the outlet channel a moderate outflow of fresh water seeps over the shingle bar. Then, with the flooding of the incoming tide, the breakers approach menacingly until at last the first blue water swirls into the narrow channel and into the inner lagoon.

From then on the sea takes over, coming in like a tidal bore, making it dangerous even to wade knee-deep in what five minutes previously were placid lake waters. The trout are awaiting this signal. The resident brown trout congregate and mass at the inner end of the outlet channel to feed on the smelt and whitebait that often pour in on the incoming tide. But – marvel of marvels – the smelt and whitebait are virtually herded and chased into the narrow channel by huge silvery sea-run trout straight in from the sea.

There is no mistaking the two types of trout the lagoon holds, but both forms are brown trout of wild stock. All derive from progeny of those introduced in 1870 from the British Isles via Tasmania. But these Waituna fresh sea-run fish are like Atlantic salmon – and often as big – powerful and silvery but for widely separated black, almost cruciform spots. They run up to 20 pound or more in weight; ten-pounders are commonplace; the average about four to five. But local wisdom is that the fishing, whilst good, is not easy. Fishless days are not uncommon. There are occasional bonanza days, but for the most part perseverance is required.

The resident fish is perhaps a wilier creature, invariably dark-backed in camouflage against the lakebed; heavily spotted and flanked with orange on golden flanks. Perhaps the resident is rather leaner in the shoulder than its sea-going brother and anything from three to twelve pounds in weight.

No one knows why some should be sea-run while others of the same stock appear to be permanent lake dwellers. Neither is the sea-run phenomenon a clear-cut annual spawning migration into fresh water, nor are they simply estuarial brown trout conditioned to tidal pools.

These Waituna sea trout come and go with the tides according to some yet undiscovered plan or evolutionary whim. They may go out again on the ebb of the same tide on which they came in on the flood. They may stay for awhile, or they may stay forever. Yet others of their tribe appear to have no sea-going instinct or inclination. Waituna Lagoon may possibly be unique in New Zealand in having intermittent but regular access to the sea. Since the very first days of acclimatisation of brown trout more than a century ago there was ample evidence of sea-going tendencies from the parent streams wherever direct and contiguous access to the sea was easy and relatively short in distance. The brown trout first liberated in the Water of Leith in Dunedin in 1868 were for the first time opened to legal fishing in 1874. Despite an initial period affording excellent fishing, by 1879 the numbers of trout being caught had declined drastically. Meanwhile, commercial fishermen operating in the extensive harbour waters between Dunedin and Port Chalmers and on out to the high seas of the South Pacific were netting ever increasing numbers of large trout with all the characteristics of sea trout. That this was strictly illegal did not prevent it happening. William Senior was in all probability New Zealand's very first fishing tourist. He recorded that the market fish stalls of Dunedin were heavy with large brown trout, showing all the characteristics of sea trout, during his visit in 1879.

It all harked back to 1864 in the London docks when the sailing ship *Norfolk* was about to depart for Hobart carrying a specific consignment of 118,000 fertilised Atlantic salmon ova under the care of James Youl. This was the second attempt to establish Atlantic salmon in the rivers off Tasmania, Victoria, and New Zealand by the burgeoning Acclimatisation Societies in the new colonies. But the sole thrust was to acclimatise salmon: no thought had been given to trout.

On the day before the ship sailed from London, while Youl was making final preparations and about to batten down his precious cargo of 118,000 eyed Atlantic salmon ova packed in moss lined boxes stowed in the specially constructed ice house on deck, there arrived on board (independently of one another and, one suspects, with considerable rivalry between them) Francis Francis and Frank Buckland. Francis brought 1500 fertilised brown trout ova and Buckland 1200. Francis's contribution was planned to total 3000 ova and was so described in most of the original documents, but it was a last minute race to obtain them before the *Norfolk* sailed from London, and Buckland was able to secure no more than 1200 ova in the allotted time.

After considerable persuasion Youl agreed to take onboard

the two separate boxes. He was far from happy about it as his terms of reference were to bring back Atlantic salmon ova, not those of brown trout. But as the relative numbers made the trout ova shipment pale to insignificance beside the total 118,000 salmon ova, and there was just about enough space left, he somewhat reluctantly agreed.

Francis Francis's contribution came from trout taken from the River Wey, at Alton in Hampshire, and from the River Wycombe, at High Wycombe in Buckinghamshire. Both were from mill streams. Those from Buckland came from a single pair of brown trout, taken by Buckland himself, from Admiral Keppel's water on a branch of the River Itchen at Bishopstoke, near Winchester.

As for the subsequent sea trout-brown trout controversy (shades of which are still argued about) Buckland claimed that the ova he collected were definitely those of the then called common (brown) trout; whereas those supplied by Francis Francis were, he believed, of sea trout. Frank Buckland was proud of the part he had played in this operation and wrote later: 'Common trout are now plentiful in Australia and New Zealand, and I believe I may fairly say that these colonies owe the existence and almost abundance of trout at the antipodes to myself.' He then described how he caught the fish and how, when he took the ova to the docks, Youl was '. . . . nearly pitching them overboard into the dirty water of the docks.' He then added: 'It was but fair to say that Mr Francis Francis at the same time sent Youl some eggs, but these were, I believe, those of the Bouge or sea-trout, not of the common trout . . .' Although Buckland subsequently withdrew this statement, and in the light of the new received wisdom that the sea trout is merely one form of the brown trout, *Salmo trutta*, he remained convinced that the sea-going tendencies of the trout hatched at Hobart, and of their subsequent progeny in New Zealand, was due entirely to Francis Francis's contribution of migratory sea trout ova.

Francis, editor of the prestigious *The Field* magazine, noted author and famed as a fisherman, thought Buckland to be too over-enthusiastic in an amateurish way; too much a popularizer, and far too much a showman. That Buckland was eccentric, to say the least, seems obvious; but the then and continued antagonism between the two men only clouded the eventual issue and made it seem far more important than it really was.

In some respects, seen now with the gift of hindsight, both men suffered from wounded vanities and in some respects at least were rather behind the current times in matters of the scientific classification of fishes – especially of trout. It would be another twenty years before Francis Day in his *British & Irish Salmonidae* (1887) would do much to quash the endless speciation that had gone on in earlier years. There were brown trout (*Salmo trutta*), sea trout (*Salmo fario*), Loch Leven trout, ferox, gillaroo, brook trout, lake trout – some with, some without Latin classification names that seemed to bring each supposedly different species established scientific authority. Then, as now, there was pseudo-science. For obvious reasons there always had been variation in local names: as in sewin, whitling, herling, and so on; but these were never intended to convey that the fish so named were of separate species. The passion for speciation was a Victorian naturalist's hobby. The fact was that, at least within the waters of the British Isles and Europe in general there was but one single species: brown trout (*Salmo trutta*), and all the very many differences between them were ones wholly derived from environment, habits, tendencies, and opportunities.

Salmo trutta is as variable a fish as man is a mammal. Once believed to be one of a large number of separate species, when anglers and scientists spoke of Loch Leven Trout, Brook Trout, Estuary Trout, Orkney Trout, Gillaroo Trout, Great Lake Trout, Salmon Trout, Sea Trout, and so on ad infinitum, although by 1864 many of the leading ichthyologists of the day were agreed that all the anadromous sea trout and non-migratory freshwater forms were simply varieties of one common species, *Salmo trutta*. Yet the old idea of separate species persists even to the present day. One should not be too surprised then that to Francis Francis and to Frank Buckland brown trout and sea trout were separate species.

Insofar as the brown trout in New Zealand are concerned, despite several later introductions and the addition from time to time of new and different genetic characteristics, they are virtually all descended from the shipments to Canterbury in 1867 and to Otago the following year. These, of course, came from stock introduced there descended from the progeny of the 1864 shipment by the *Norfolk* from London to Hobart.

It is apparent from reading the old accounts that after the safe hatching of the first trout in the ponds at Plenty near the Derwent Estuary at Hobart, and of ova from the descendents of these fish a few years later in Christchurch in New Zealand, that the newly introduced trout prospered and grew on faster than expected, but all struck out seawards if there was any chance of access away from their natal streams. In other words, both in the Canterbury rivers and in the rivers of Otago, as well as those subsequently released into streams and lakes in Southland, virtually all tended to run down to the sea if given the opportunity. And very much it remains so to this day.

This does not mean, of course, that it proves there is a separate species of sea trout, distinct from brown trout in inherited characteristics. There may be elements of this in the genetic make up of the entire New Zealand stock of brown trout, but it rather goes to show that the ichthyologists are correct: how plastic a species the brown trout really is; a creation of its own particular environment.

But, as was the case in Britain, local variations due to water chemistry, available food supplies, the type and nature of the streams themselves, together with many other variables, soon began to produce local variations in the subsequent progenies of the New Zealand acclimatised tribes of self-sustaining, wild populations of brown trout – *Salmo trutta* – in all his wide

78

range of varieties.

The reader is asked to forgive that ichthyological diversion in what set out to be a simple narrative tale of fishing. But fish and fishing are never just simple, nor may a tale of fishing be no more than narrative of a particular day. Whatever else they may have thought about the nothing short of phenomenal growth and success in the establishment of the trout in New Zealand one thing is certain. Neither Francis Francis nor Frank Buckland could have dreamed there would one day be a race of seagoing trout as came to dwell in Waituna Lagoon, narrowly skirting the pounding surf of the Southern Ocean, and often breached by its powerful tides and awesome Roaring Forties storms.

When the outlet is open to the sea after a southerly storm and the tide surges in, the visual impact is quite remarkable to behold. My own first visit to the place was made many years ago, by foot rather than by trailer-launched dinghy as favoured by virtually all local and knowledgeable anglers. Angling pressure is light throughout most parts of the South Island and lightens even more as a trout fisherman moves southwards. Waituna Lagoon is as far south as it is possible to go; the southernmost trout fishery of all.

It is lightly fished, mostly by a small band of dedicated locals who might even be considered slightly eccentric. With much more highly extolled stream fishing nearby it almost never attracts visiting fly-fishermen and, in any case, few fishermen at all ever start out from the small port of Bluff as I did. It is just as well I did not know the going would be so hard, otherwise I probably would never have attempted it. And the locals, who make the journey by boat, may do so more comfortably and quicker, but in so doing miss out on what was one of the most unique experiences of my fishing life.

I had driven a hire car from my ship at Bluff, through the outskirts of Invercargill, and out along the country road to the small farming settlement of Kapuka. From here an even lesser road takes one south again towards the extreme southern coast of the South Island and to Waituna Lagoon. Although Waituna does have its few regular fishermen who no doubt swear by the place – and equally, by no doubt, at it at times – being situate, as it is, about midway between two famed and fabled trout rivers – the Oreti and the Mataura – most anglers give it a miss.

The track road finishes close by the far eastern end of the lagoon. It is neither particularly impressive nor beautiful hereabouts. An insignificant creek drains into the narrow, shallow end of the lagoon. From here a short track leads out to the shingle spit enclosing the lagoon itself from the sea. Once on the shingle it is as trackless as the Sahara and, in some places, just as hard going. For awhile I alternated between walking along the lagoon shore, always prospecting for places to fish, then scrambling up over the often high-banked ridge of piled up shingle to walk close by along the ocean beach. For the first few miles it is possible to alternate one's route because the shingle bank is so narrow and easily traversed. But closer to the outlet itself, almost six miles onwards, the spit widens considerably and the going gets heavy, so that the walking track along the seaward side takes one away from the lagoon but quicker by far towards the outlet.

I was at least equipped for the journey, albeit laden down like a pack mule: shod in stout walking boots, with rubber thigh waders slung across my shoulders; a back-pack heavy with tackle and provisions, and a spinning rod (as I had been advised to take along by a chance informant incredulous that I had intentions of tramping to the sea outlet), in addition to my more favoured fly rod.

I knew from intelligence received that the outlet was thought to have been breached in a hard blow and spring tide the previous day. The storm itself had moved on, eastwards, passing on into the South Pacific from the great Southern Ocean, but a stiff onshore wind blew all the same, and a thundering surf pounded on to the debris strewn beach. The air

80

was wet and cold with sea-spray and the salt stung my face as I walked into it. After a few miles I climbed up over the high shingle dune, looking down across the lagoon spread out before me; almost calm after the thundering wind and sea on the ocean side. It didn't take much to persuade myself to divert from my true objective, and slide down the shingle bank to the shore of the lagoon. Suddenly, out of the wind and cut off from the rumbling and incessant noise of the sea, it was calm, silent and warm in the early October spring sunshine. The salt spray had encrusted on my face, so I washed it off in the peaty, slightly brackish water of the lagoon, then set up my fly rod and took stock of the surroundings. The ruins of a one-time fence ran out into the water, and across on the far side the same fence line continued up into a disused overgrown, forlorn paddock. It had the look of a fishy, trouty spot. A breeze nicely ruffled the water; sheltered here by the high shingle bank behind me, so that the wind itself was diverted as it followed the shape and outline of the lagoon; blowing nicely from the west with a pretty ripple dancing over the water. There was not another soul in sight: indeed I had seen no one since parking my car at the very end of the road earlier that morning.

In those days I almost always started out fly-fishing in such a new place with a sinking line and a Red Setter fly, which is the only reason I can now remember it. Casting out across the sunlit water was pleasant therapy and a change from slogging and slushing around ankle deep in shifting shingle. Some time later, lulled by the rhythm of casting and retrieve, I must have fallen (as I am wont to do) into a reverie that took my mind off the more serious aspects of fly-fishing, so that when the fish took the fly I had to strip line in hard to gain contact. Then the trout turned away, heading out across the lagoon, stripping off fly line almost to the backing.

There were no histrionics on the part of the fish; no great leaps out of the water, no tailwalking; just a series of solid deep-boring runs, one after the other, but strong and heavy, so

81

that the rod tip trembled and the fly line thrummed in my fingers and as it came back on to the temporary safety of the reel. It was a clear and easy shore on which to beach the fish. I backed up the scrubby shingle bank, rod high, gathering speed on the short line outside the rod tip and the trout followed on, coming with me, but still shaking and complaining from time to time so that I knew I needed to be quick with him. He slid up on to the beach as nicely as any trout has ever done for me, and with a turn I was between him and the water and with a flick he was high and dry and safely ashore. I fell to admiring my prize, even while I killed it.

It was a perfectly formed and marked brown trout and weighed in at exactly five pounds. In those days I still weighed every fish I caught, whether to kill or return to the water. As a then ongoing habit this ceremony of weighing and sometimes measuring was a rite performed as part of the numeracy by which, I suppose, in those days, I still measured fishing itself.

This trout was golden and buttery yellow, with black and orange spots flanking a darker back. It looked like nothing but a resident, home-loving brown trout, and lovely though it was, had none of the verve and panache of an obviously sea-run fish. I buried the trout in soft, wet sandy shingle, marking his temporary resting place with a stick to which I tied a short length of twine, like a pennant, because I am notorious for burying or otherwise hiding trout and never being able to find them again; a bad habit I was delightfully relieved of when, a few years on, I ceased altogether to kill trout.

It seemed a good time and place to eat sandwiches and drink a welcome can of beer, before getting on my way again, resuming the long walk along the seaward shingle spit towards the lagoon outlet. From here on I followed the track on the southern seaward side, and it was here I first passed a lonely spume sodden surfcaster fishing into the breakers. The going was easier now – or perhaps I was simply getting used to it – yet completing the long tramp seemed to take for ever, and reaching the narrow gut of the outlet came as a sudden surprise to me because there were three or four fishermen on foot, spread out along the steep shingle bank through which the incoming tide was roaring in like a maelstrom. Further inside, close to the minimum allowable distance of half a kilometre, there were two small aluminium dinghies with outboards, each containing two fishermen. But by comparison with the earlier part of my day the place seemed overcrowded and, although spectacular, not nearly so inviting a place to fish.

This was no dry fly water, any more than it was any place for a fly rod. Open to the thundering sea, swell, and roaring incoming flood tide, the wind was strong, coming straight in from the south and feeling as if it had come straight from Antarctica. This roaring mass of water at the outlet is perhaps moving in at ten knots or more; tumbling, eddying, whirlpooling, then with each withdrawal of the breaking surf a surge sets up in the opposite direction going seawards. The noise alone of the shifting shingle, and the undeflected sea wind, together with the roar of breaking water, was deafening. The combination of it all was quite exhilarating and tremendously exciting to fish.

I followed local fashion and set up a light spinning rod, a fixed spool reel loaded with about nine-pound test monofilament and a silver-wedge wobbler lure. This was heavy enough to cast into a strong wind and to get down in the swirling mass of water on a fast retrieve.

The water was always moving, but there were occasional lulls when suddenly the surface water seemed less turbulent, and I could see here and there the great backs of big trout herding in the smelt and whitebait into which they charged headlong in a crazy sort of abandon.

The angler fishing just seawards of me was into a fish within minutes of my arrival, and within minutes of that had, almost nonchalantly, beached a beautiful silvery sea-run hen trout of eleven pounds. Another fisherman walked towards the place and with a desultory flick cast his lure into the seething mass of water and was immediately fast into another hard-running trout. He beached an equally silvery six-pounder. These were nothing like the trout I had caught a few miles into the quiet waters of the sheltered lagoon, yet they were recognisably the same fish despite the differences of plasticity created by their environments – so close together, yet seemingly so different in environmental habit. The trout I had caught had all the hallmarks of a resident brown in fine condition, and looked as if it had never so much as sniffed salt water. Yet these two fish I saw taken in quick succession were silvery bright; every inch of them straight in from the sea, as if the tumbling surf and salt water was their natural and proper habitat.

I stopped for a mug of thermos coffee, thankful for the comparative seawards lee created by a depression in the shingle, no doubt caused by some earlier southerly storm. Here in this relatively sheltered spot I was approached by another fisherman who, being a local farmer and knowing all the regulars there, knew me to be a visiting stranger. He was surprised to see that I had even got to such an isolated inaccessible place, let alone that I had tramped to it from the road at the far eastern end. I was made very welcome and given much local expert knowledge of how best to fish this strange place.

This man – his name, he told me, was Tom Gilmour – was appalled to hear I intended tramping back to my car that evening. He and his uncle had come up by boat, fishing at various places on the way, and now fishing the incoming tide from the shore. They planned to leave in about an hour from then, and offered me a lift back down the lagoon, so that the thought of not having to go through the ankle-shuddering shingle-sliding of the return journey filled me with sudden comfort – and he would drop into the bay by the ruined fence, where I had buried my fish, so that I might collect it.

I am not a fishing diarist in the usual sense, but do have a little notebook in which I recorded fishing expeditions at about that time. It was Friday the 8th of October. Tom

Gilmour told me that on Opening Day, exactly a week earlier, he had taken a 20 pound precisely fresh sea- run brown from just inside the main channel. The fish was 38 inches long and just over 19 inches in girth. Obviously not all the trout there incoming from the sea on the tide do so in a fine feeding frenzy. This particular fish had not fed for some time and it was estimated it would have topped 22 pounds had it been doing so. But even at 20 pounds exactly, it was the record brown trout to have been taken from Waituna.

Fortified by Tom Gilmour's words, and the prospect of an easy trip back to the car, I resumed fishing: this time right at the inner end of the short, canal-like breach through the shingle arm enclosing the lagoon. There was more shelter here from the wind, and I was able to cast further, into a wide, swirling pool of heavy, tumbling water, heaving, confused, and troubled with surging back-eddies, as if all the water already inside the lagoon was desperately seeking to get out again, back to the storm-tossed sea.

I am not overfond of spinning as a form of fishing, and find the repeated mechanical actions too empty of the subtle nuances of casting a fly, as a result of which I tend to lose concentration; and certainly did on that occasion. It was no different from what seemed exactly the same as the previous hundred or so. Except that this time the line tautened and sang, the rod bent low, and the reel gave out line with that engaging sweetness so particular to a small fixed spool reel, as the hooked fish leapt high into the air, then streaked away towards the far shore.

For awhile all went well. Each time I gained more line than was lost on the following run. What I hadn't taken sufficient notice of was that in this mass of water – racing in through the central channel, and tumbling out in swirling back eddies before rejoining and consolidating the inwards rush – there was much floating sea kelp and ocean debris. I had seen the occasional three or four foot length of waterlogged, almost completely submerged small tree and bush tops – like forlorn

Christmas trees – but hadn't countered being entangled in one between me and the fish.

The trout was running hard in the central current but, with an alarming bow in the line in the opposite direction caused by the whirlpooling back eddy, with the considerable dead weight of the waterlogged tree branch immediately making the situation nothing short of precarious, I knew it was most unlikely I could now land the fish. From now on I was fighting the waterlogged tree branch, not the trout; while the trout was fighting the tree branch itself, not me.

I would have liked to have beached that sea-run brown, but it was not to be on that particular day. It was a relief, in a way, when I knew the line between the submerged branch and the fish had parted; the branch simply came in towards the shingle, lying in the lesser current, and I broke it off with a sigh. How big would that sea-run trout have been? Six? Eight? Ten? Twelve pounds? Maybe more? I shall never know, but sometimes still wonder.

Soon afterwards we were chortling down the lagoon in Tom Gilmour's outboard powered aluminium dinghy – a lift I was indeed most grateful. The shingle had taken its toll on my ankles even by then. We picked up my trout, and while I was exhuming it from its temporary burial place by the lakeshore Tom's uncle had a few casts while still sitting in the boat and got a lively three-pounder.

And so ended my day: as different a fishing day as I had ever experienced. It was fishing in a wild place. I made my way back to Bluff, well satisfied with the day.

Because I had planned to do so anyway, I went back to Waituna Lagoon the following day, rather than make a trip to the Oreti. It was a good day, but not the same. Sore and tired ankles, and occasional driving cold rain showers from the south, put me off the prospect of the long tramp back to the outlet. I had at least been there once, and experienced its strange and awesome grandeur.

So, instead, I went back to the fence line and fished less frenetically, feeling happier and more at ease with a fly rod. It was a good day and worthy of another visit. I had hooked and lost a good fish earlier in the day, but in mid-afternoon, just in fact about the time I was thinking of making an early end to it, and at the far extremity of a long cast and the first tightening tweak of my retrieve, there was an eruption of water as the hooked fish leapt into the sparkling sunlight. From then on it was all submarine on the trout's part, but it was a strong fish and had no natural inclination to come in to the bank, although it permitted me to walk it like a dog on a lead for about fifty yards along the beach towards a better landing spot where it was duly beached.

Much to my delight it was a fresh sea-run brown, all silvery bright, short, thick shouldered, glistening, gorgeously arrayed and a delight to my heart. It was a shade over eight pounds and 26 inches in length. With that I did make an end to it and came away a happy man indeed.

A TALE OF TWO RIVERS

. . . . . we came to the Waipunga Falls – my first
experience of great waterfalls – they are indescrib-
ably beautiful – three – one beside the other – and a
ravine of bush either side – The noise like thunder
and the sun shone full on the water – I am sitting
now on the bank of the river – just a few yards
away – the water is flowing past – and the manuka
flax and fern line the banks . . . .

Katherine Mansfield, *The Urewera Notebook*

The Waipunga River lies in the very heart of the central
North Island of New Zealand. As far as geographers are
concerned it is one river, rising in the first foothills in the far
southeast corner of the great Kaingaroa Plain and Forest, but
running almost due south, away from the exotic forest to track
through a narrow valley, cutting through swathes of native
bush before opening out into a wider valley floor where it
meanders through pumice country in successions of faster
water and the newer arms of once oxbow lakes in its saunter-
ing to what I call the very end of the first Waipunga.

At this point the river narrows and speeds up its progress,
then – close by the Taupo-Napier road – issues from a great
rocky cleft, cascading over the scenic Waipunga Falls, down
through a great vertical cliff of stone before tumbling into a
deep pool below – then rushing off again as a newborn, fast

bubbly, rocky river, so different in character from the river above the falls. This is the second Waipunga of my tale.

Not only are these two parts of the Waipunga River so very different in character and nature, they have for fly fishermen another aspect of uniqueness. Above the falls there dwells a race of brown trout famed even in a land where brown trout are ubiquitous and plentiful. Below the falls there dwells a race of rainbow trout famed even in a land where rainbow trout are just as ubiquitous and plentiful. Separated by the sheer, vertical face of the Waipunga Falls the two different species of trout are not only kept apart from any intermingling and subsequent competition but, to all intents and purposes, inhabit two very different rivers. It provides for a fascinating exercise in the matter of a day's fishing: fishing for brown trout in the morning (when the sunlight is best for spotting the fish on upstream nymphing); then going below the falls for lunch, before fishing up through the totally different pools and fast rocky runs of the lower river for its resident rainbows. There are some browns in the lower river, but for the most part this is not brown trout water, and I for one have never caught one there. The lower river, below the falls, is rainbow water typified.

The Waipunga is a major tributary of the mightier Mohaka River, famed for its brown trout and rainbows, and perhaps the only major river in New Zealand with an established run of sea-going rainbows, where on the Hawkes Bay coast at least some of the rainbow stock have reverted to their racially inherited steelhead instincts. Upstream, however, in the Waipunga of which I now write, right in the heart of the North Island, the browns and rainbows are truly resident and do not wander far or wide.

My good friends John Parsons and Bill Crawford were the first to devise a plan for fishing the Waipunga. In the manner in which Ben Hur Lampman meant that every fisherman should have a secret river – a river he can call his own – so is this river for John and Bill. John feels protective about it. He goes back to it again and again. It is a river he can't keep away from; and doesn't want to, anyway. Without seeming to be in any way overtly metaphysical about it, I would even say that he goes to this particular river of his as in going to a shrine. If the reader doesn't understand what I mean by saying that, then it doesn't matter. I can't say it any better without sounding crass. If, on the other hand, the reader does know what I mean, then there is no need to say any more. All is clear without getting into linguistic conundrums. Bill, too, loves this stream dearly, and knows it better than any man; almost every inch of it. He, too, is protective about it, and it angers him when he sees this potentially fragile mountain stream abused and despoiled, as it sometimes is, by louts and vandals with nets and setlines and worse.

In this respect Bill is secretive about the river and sometimes fears for its continuance as one of the finest trout streams in New Zealand. There is nothing very private about the lower river, below the falls, because the highway from Taupo to Napier follows it for several miles, albeit that the road lies above steep and convoluted ravines and access is not for the faint-hearted. The upper river, however, is in itself a very secret place. It runs through often flat tussocky pumice country, underlying striking white cliffs in places, while elsewhere it meanders in great oxbow loops through stands of brushy manuka and streamside flax, toitoi, and the ubiquitous, painful, stinging Spaniard.

So convoluted are some of these loops and bends that they take on something of the awareness of a natural maze. The manuka is generally about six or seven feet in height, so that walking through it one can easily become quite lost and disoriented. I know, for it has often happened to me. With nothing to take bearings of, and an astonishing sense of confusion – because it is one of those places with an almost overwhelming sense of place – it is often possible to stay calm and very quiet and listen for the silvery tinkle and magic gurgling sound of the river itself, murmuring away in talking to itself as it flows along. Then from within the featureless jungle of manuka scrub one strikes out towards the sound of the singing river.

In some stretches of the upper river the oxbow loops are so very nearly through a complete circle, followed by a short, straight run, or a deeper pool, that it is possible to go down to the river at some known approach, then fish upstream for an hour or two through a bewildering array of different types of water, always following the river itself, yet come out at the end of it only a short distance – perhaps a few hundred yards – along the pumice track from where one went in.

It can have a most disconcerting effect on the angler. You park your car by a clearing off the rough pumice road, where it ends before continuing as a hunters' and trampers' track into the hills, then go down to a clearly visible watercress-fringed pool nearby. From there upstream, there is more than enough fine nymphing and dry fly water – all varied, in a succession of runs and pools and hairpin bends – to provide a careful fly fisherman with three or four hours of fishing, yet emerge at the end of it barely a few hundred yards up the track from where he first went in. It has the effect of making it seem that one has simply emerged from another world. At first, of course, this strange feeling and odd awareness only comes on coming out from the place; but as one gets to know the place there is the same knowledge and awareness on each first stepping into it, as if one is thus entering that other private, different world inside the watery maze.

In much the same way, once emerging from the twisting loops and mysteries of the stream, time itself takes a tumble and a twist. It is not only a matter of where have I been, but of why the time it took now seems telescoped; that it seemed to take so long.

Despite the circuitous loops of the river, the morning light is best and kinder for stalking trout. While it is possible to fish this part of the river blind, simply casting dry fly or nymph up into likely holding places, it is much more satisfying as well as rewarding to stalk the banks with all the caution of a hunter.

There are times when in certain lights the trout may be sighted in plain splendour, out on a sandy pumice bar on the inner edge of a pool – often more than one trout in strict territorial positioning. But at other times, in other places, only a faint and vague tell-tale sign will indicate a trout's holding position: sometimes the unmistakable distortion of water close by a throbbing tail; at other times a mere suspicion of a trout being there; at other times still the trout's own shadow reflected off the bottom. But, unless you stalk with all the cunning of an Indian, all you will see is the trout scurrying off in haste, having seen or heard you first, after which you might as well forget about fishing thereabouts for at least half an hour, even more.

Under Bill's tutelage over many years I, who by nature tends to be clumsy, learned much about stalking trout, although I remained handicapped by a decided lack of the finer sensibilities. Bill is the best spotter and stalker of trout I have ever known. He has an uncanny ability in this matter. Often he becomes aware of a trout's presence and exact position, not because he had actually seen it first, but because he noticed something not quite normal about his view of a particular place. Perhaps the refractions, reflections, and the tricks of light through fronds and curls of moving, running water seemed not exactly right. Maybe there were dappled shadows on underwater rocks that ought not have been there, in that particular place, unless they were caused by an unseen trout. Then, having as it were divined the presence of a trout, he would see it – while I, perhaps, despite his careful pointing of it out to me, could still not see it. And in this fashion I often fished for big brown trout in the Waipunga and similar New Zealand streams, sighted by Bill, and fished for by me under his direction as to where and how to cast. I might have got a little better at it over the years, but was blind compared with Bill Crawford. He had a rare faculty for doing so.

So rare, in fact, that on one occasion I was with him, and he had taken along as a guest a famous visiting overseas fly-fishing swami and author, noted in the world of fishing for his ability to spot trout. The narrow path wound close by the stream. Bill said, quite ingenuously and modestly, 'We should be able to spot two or three trout along this stretch. I'll lead the way and show you where and when I've sighted a good trout, then you can have a go for it.'

The visiting swami didn't seem impressed, but followed on close behind Bill, while I came along at the rear, several yards behind them. After going a slow and cautious hundred yards or so, and much as I'd expected, Bill suddenly stopped, advising caution with a raised hand, and hidden behind a toitoi clearly indicated exactly where the sighted trout lay out in the stream, inviting the visitor to go for it. The distinguished swami cupped his hands over his long-peaked cap, adjusted his polaroids, and announced he could see no trout; that there was no trout there. But he did have a few exceedingly well executed and competent casts over the lie of the fish. Then Bill said, 'OK. He's gone. You spooked him that time. We'll move on.'

The swami responded by saying he didn't think a fish had been there in the first place. Bill gave me the sort of smile that only Bill can give at such a time. We moved on upstream. Almost the same sequence of events took place, after which the overseas swami said, 'Look, Bill, I've been stalking trout for as many years as you've lived. I don't think you are seeing fish. I'll go first and spot for myself.'

Our Indian file continued on upstream, except that now the swami led the way, crouching low, always watching for the tell-tale sign of a trout. His pace actually quickened, and when it was suggested to him that he should slow down, he replied that there were no trout in those stretches, anyway, and if there was a trout he would certainly see it.

We continued on upstream with no halting the swami, although he went through the motions of careful looking. Occasionally along the track Bill would turn around to me and, with a wicked smile on his face, such as only Bill can give, would indicate to me in his clear but sparse, coded riverbank gestures exactly where a trout lay in full plain sight out there in the stream, but which our distinguished visitor had passed on by.

We must have covered a mile of the upper Waipunga, in which even I, a poor stalker of trout, had also actually sighted at least four of the eight large brown trout Bill had secretly pointed out to me, unknown to our guest who led the single file. Suddenly, the swami announced, 'No trout here. Might as well go somewhere else. Thought you said it would be full of trout.'

'Can't recall saying it would be full of trout,' said Bill, 'but I did spot eight coming up immediately behind you.'

'Nonsense,' said the swami. 'Not a single trout anywhere along that stream. I've been spotting trout all my life. I know. Let's go somewhere else.'

I didn't mention to him that even I had sighted four of the eight brown trout Bill had pointed out to me, and with a conservative guess I'd say that none of them was less than about four pounds. So, he went away convinced that the upper Waipunga was a troutless river, and this he knew because he was an acknowledged swami.

Heavy rains up in the hills can colour the river, although for the most part the Waipunga is gin clear in the way that much used expression gin clear is supposed to mean, but rarely does. But the hills, up where the source waters spring, are of soft, almost sandy pumice, and the river is sometimes sparkling with suspended pumice dust, each minute speck of which scintillates with kaleidoscopic prismatic golden lights like bubbles in champagne.

Fly-fishing for trout is far from ritualized in New Zealand. As a sport in that country it is far too freely available and universally excellent in quality to be in any danger of falling into lasting dogma or ritualisation. And by this, I mean, not the often quoted ritualisation and dogma of the post-Halfordian ethic on the chalkstreams of southern England, but the newer and far worse dogmas of the competition-driven and motivated, catch-a-limit-at-all-costs philosophy of so many contemporary stillwater trout fisheries. Even worse, perhaps, is the technique-driven ritualisation of such fishing itself, in which there seems no mention or awareness of the sheer joys and pleasures of just going fishing.

No. New Zealand is gladly without such ritualisation. But it does have its private rituals, and I took part in one such, right here on the Waipunga. It is sometimes hard to extend the sense of the joy of fly-fishing in a land so blessed with first-class trout waters of world renown, simply because it happens so commonly among virtually all types and conditions of people, and is generally so universally available. Even in areas where winter fishing is permissible, and often the best of the year in terms of limit bags, it is not necessarily followed with any enthusiasm by all anglers. The little group with whom I fished, who all lived in Taupo, but only occasionally or sometimes never actually fished in Taupo waters, developed certain rituals based upon the fisherman's seasons, or on how the fisherman's seasons used to be.

We always celebrated Opening Day as a joyous event – and it always was. We used to celebrate Closing Day, heralding the end of another fishing season, although for some of us the taking down of our fly rods was a symbolic act, rather than a final one, because a few of us could not be induced by that unassuaged lust for fishing to forego a personally undertaken close season in waters that were closed, to fish the winter runs of rainbows in the Tongariro when the fishing there was not only permissible, but at its best.

Perhaps even more of a ritual was the annual Boxing Day fishing outing. Often in the streams of which I write, three fly-fishermen together constituted a crowd, and two were deemed better. But, on Boxing Day, that dictum would be ignored. Perhaps as many as eight of us would fill two or three cars on that first day after Christmas and head for the hills and a favourite trout stream – the Waipunga – in unseemly gregariousness for eight people who generally wished to fish alone, or with one other companion.

We would all take cold turkey, cold chicken, salads, baguettes, mince pies, nuts, Christmas cake: often enough to have fed a small army. And one such Boxing Day in particular I remember so fondly we made the pilgrimage to the Waipunga. To fish the upper river in the morning for brown trout, then go down to the lower river below the falls after lunch to fish the sparkling faster waters for rainbows.

It was a good day. The weather was fine, but the river was bespeckled with pumice and upstream debris. Normally we had a deluge of rain on our Boxing Day visit.

For readers who do not know the country let it be said that New Zealand goes outdoors at Christmas. It is not only the biggest holiday time of the year, but half the population of the North Island appear to converge on Taupo, from Auckland to the north, Wellington to the south, Napier to the east, and New Plymouth to the west. Taupo – normally a quietish sort of resort, holiday town – virtually fills up. There would have been standing room only in the Waitahanui, and only then after queueing up to get in, but not many miles away up in the hills on the Waipunga we didn't see another soul all day.

Fortunately for me in this present writing my friend John Parsons has written of this particular day in his book *Parsons' Passion* – A Troutfisher's Year, Halcyon Press, Auckland, 1990 – a book, unfortunately, only generally well known and available in New Zealand. Normally none of us mixed fishing and drinking but, the designated car drivers excepted, the rest of us imbibed fairly well that day, so John's account of the day's fishing is certainly more detailed than anything I might recollect. He called this particular chapter of *Parsons' Passion*, 'Another Joyful Day':

Brian's fish lay in its usual place. Well, not quite usual; instead of sheltering behind the small-rock jumble it had taken up station just ahead of it, and

this was strange. I would have thought the flow of fine pumice and other debris bombarding it in today's high-level medium murk would have kept it snugly behind the barrier.

No matter; here was a visible fish at last on this otherwise blind-fishing day; a fish discovered only because I knew it ought to be there; the fish Brian knows so well.

I'd tunnelled through the buttercups and daisies and tall seeding summer grasses to satisfy myself that the fish was in residence. Half a metre out from the trailing toitoi leaves, it held station, moving slowly up and down and sideways to field small living things among the debris.

Then it rose to take something off the surface. And again.

'Try a Green Beetle!' I bawled at Bryn beyond the toitoi bush downstream. 'And then tell me when you're ready!' Perfection, as Bryn rightly observes, is an illusion.

This day came as close to perfection, weatherwise, as ever one is likely to encounter. But if only the river had remained the river Colin and I fished three weeks ago! Then, clear and just below medium flow, we'd fastened on to rainbows and browns in many of the places we chose to fish. Then, because the season was not quite far enough advanced for terrestrials to have brought fish to the surface, we'd fished weighted nymphs upstream. Today, when green beetles and cicadas whizzed and tumbled, the water was too high, just too turbid, to encourage fish up. All except Brian's fish.

'Ready!' shouted Bryn. 'Well, as ready as I'll ever be!'

I told him where the fish lay; suggested he land the Green Beetle under the toitoi head hanging low to the water a metre upstream of the fish.

Bryn's white line flew to and fro across my grass-surrounded field of vision. Suddenly, a high toitoi head above the fish jumped forward, and stayed there. Loud and rude words fell on my ears until the fly, miraculously for anyone who knows the implacability of toitoi, came free.

'He's still there! You haven't put him down!' I shouted.

Two good casts later we concluded Green Beetle was not on the menu after all.

Bryn tied on a lightly-weighted nymph instead. Louder and ruder words coincided with his final forward cast. You know what happens. The cast never materialises because some obscene object behind you leaps up or down or across and grabs the fly.

Bryn waded across the river and freed the nymph. Next cast, abetted by a sudden breeze, another toitoi head above the fish swooped for the nymph and deftly caught it.

By the time Bryn's red-hot expletives had singed all the foliage within fifty metres and I'd reported that the fish was still feeding, God bless it, I judged that Bryn would be happier for my departure, and I went. Nothing that I could see lay feeding along the river for the next hundred metres, and I was almost up to the back-eddy pool when Brian himself appeared behind me.

'Nothing doing', he reported. 'Well, only a small one'.

'Bryn caught your fish yet?'

'Nope. Still trying.'

I guessed that's why he'd moved up from the corner pool and the frustration of murky water. Hereabouts we had just two chances, maybe three, of spotting fish. The first would be the place at which Bryn was busy defoliating the landscape. The second would be the back-eddy we were cautiously approaching. The third was only a short distance above the back-eddy where, in a fine deep run with undercut banks, Brian had recently seen a fish that made his eyes bulge.

Two fish were patrolling the back eddy just under the surface. We collapsed slowly out of sight into the grass. Suddenly, Bryn appeared, beaming, behind us. 'I got that fish! On a Humpy. Nice fish, probably four pounds,' he said modestly, so I reckon it was five.

Maybe that one is used to capture and release, because it came in like a lamb, as if aware that Bryn, like Brian (and most of us, for that matter), would play and unhook it as quickly as possible and send it on its way rejoicing.

Meanwhile, the first back-eddy fish had twice refused Brian's Royal Wulff Variant. For its sins it was then presented with a Mark II Green Beetle, which speedily homed in to a cavernous groping mouth and hung on until Brian released it five minutes later. Maybe green beetles and cicadas were only newly falling victim to that jack fish, for he was still kelt-thin, although an ugly partly-healed scar reaching down both sides of his back below the dorsal fin told of an encounter with an eel or a shag which had probably put him back a few weeks.

The other back-eddy fish was similarly wanting in the rotundity which days of green beetle and cicada feeding would give him. This one did become briefly mine, but before I could join the ranks of those who'd hooked and returned a fish that morning, a great deal of water flowed under a great many bridges.

You really have to fish the back-eddy from the

other side, especially if an occupant surface-browses well away from the edge of the current. This one was such a fish, so after the intervening current had imparted drag on the Green Beetle twice, and the fish had understandably pottered off to less alarming morsels, I waded across the river downstream and got into position upstream of the eddy.

Bryn and Brian shouted all kinds of advice and abuse from grandstand seats across the river as that infuriating fish ignored fly after fly. At one stage it took me three trembling tries to knot on one of my own little Coch-y- bondhus. The fish ignored that too.

'Cast your line across and I'll put on a Mark II Green Beetle', Brian called. 'It's got more hackle on it than the Mark I'.

I tied on one of his big Cicadas instead, and plopped it down behind the fish. The fish turned quickly, swam up to it, sneered, and resumed its leisurely sampling of other goodies.

'You tie bloody awful flies, Brian!' I shouted over to him.

'It's the fisherman, not the fly!' he smugly retorted.

Well, I settled that Cicada lightly or heavily six or eight times near that fish before he finally condescended to put me out of my misery.

I thought I'd struck too soon, but in fact the Cicada had lodged well inside his mouth when I came to free it. Even though I turned the fish upside down to take the hook out, he was determined not to stick to the rules. Instead of lying quiescent in the supine position that encourages passivity, he nearly bit my fingers off, twice. Brian and Bryn were entirely without sympathy.

I've so often fished that river on hot summer days

in full battle order and finished up exhausted that this time I travelled guerilla-light. It really is the only way to fish. I even left the flask of tea behind. And I wore, joy of joys, a pair of lightweight rubber-soled boots with green canvas uppers reaching way above the ankles. I'd been on the lookout for that kind and colour of boot for years. They were in the shops for Christmas, and were an obvious choice for Dad once I'd thrown out a hint or two.

Mind you, before the five of us had even started fishing that morning, and on the long walk back from the back-eddy to the cars for lunch, I had to ignore remarks about Twinkle Toes and Highland dancers. Someone even made disparaging remarks about my new hat. He wondered what I was doing wearing a green flower-pot.

They were all jealous, I suppose.

Lunch was a long-drawn-out affair. Our Boxing Day trout-fishing lunches invariably are. Everyone has to bring a bottle of wine, together with the rich cold pickings from Christmas Day's chicken or turkey topped off with fruit-mince pies and Christmas cake.

Today, in the blessed shade of a great beech, our party of five anglers cheerfully settled down to the business in hand. Corks were pulled in seconds. Food appeared and disappeared. Bill and Fred quickly drowned fishless sorrows. Bryn and Fred told wonderful stories which became more and more improbable as the wine-bottles emptied.

Two years before, we'd lunched in the same place while the rain hissed down. Today's weather was totally different, and though we couldn't enthuse over the state of the river we went hopefully fishing again after lunch. An hour and a half was all it took to convince ourselves that water-conditions were not what they should be. Bryn and I encountered only one fish, and only because, like the morning's ones, it was to be expected in a particular lie.

I had peered through the long grass overhanging the deep quiet edge of the pool, and there it was, busily intercepting nymphs and caddis bowling down with the pumice and detritus from the rapids above.

Bryn hooked the fish first cast. I watched the white line-end drifting past under the overhanging grasses just below me, and suddenly it stopped. Bryn struck, and the fish jumped. The pool favours hooked fish which decide to clear out downstream, and indeed it happily extended that favour once again. Bryn almost pulled it back up the fast out-flow. But not quite. The tippet broke.

We grimaced across to each other, and fished the next pool without result, and then took to the cool shade of big beeches and pongas on the way to the track back to the car.

That leafy, sun-dappled path through forest giants and forest midgets put the seal on our pleasure. We grinned at each other. It had been a joyful day.

Somehow, reading those words again, written by a good friend about a fishing day we shared, I am struck by the sort of remembrance of which it makes me most acutely aware – almost in the Proustian way of *A la recherche du temps perdu* – in ways that no words of my own might now recollect.

That last fish that broke off in the rough and broken water at the bottom of Parsons' Pool was, of course, a rainbow because, after our Boxing Day luncheon picnic we fished the lower Waipunga below the falls. This in itself was something of a ritual, for in the afternoon it was hard to spot trout in the upper river, where we had fished in the morning, and the fish I had caught there was a lovely brown trout. The fast runs and riffles of the lower river – fishing upstream and heading northwestwards – were more befitting the afternoons. One did fish into the sun, albeit, but up into rolling, roily, fast moving water that came tumbling down over a stony boulder riverbed. It was rainbow water. Pure rainbow water. No stalking fish here. Long casts up into the sparkling sunlight, tossing a lightly weighted nymph into the silvery-gold sheen of turbulent water, ever in motion, babbling and bubbling; noisy water, in fact, quite unlike the more gladey meadow waters of the upper river.

As for it being Parsons' Pool, that was all part of Bill's fondness for naming unnamed pools. On these relatively unfished backcountry mountain streams the pools and runs had no known names, so Bill named them as he went along; rather in the manner in which the Australian Aborigines of the Centre sing their landscapes into existence by naming everything they encounter along their songlines. In such a fashion, Bill sang the pools and riffles of secret rivers into true meaning. Thus, on various rivers in the central North Island, quite apart from Parsons' Pool we have just visited, there was Winstone's Revenge, where Winstones – a New Zealand equivalent of Wimpey or Tarmac – having completed building several road bridges over one wild and turbulent river had built a reinforced concrete revetment below one such bridge, and somehow, instead of carrying away the surplus and broken concrete blocks appear to have dumped them along the way into one such excellent fishing pool. It still provided fine fishing for rainbow trout, although the natural landscape was somewhat disfigured, but the iron reinforcing bars in the broken concrete blocks stuck out and were often deadly underwater traps spread around towards the head of the pool. Even if they didn't come close to breaking a wading angler's ankles, they would often puncture his waders, or make getting in or out of the water seem like an assault course. Hence, with Bill's wry humour, the pool was named Winstone's Revenge, or plain Winstone's.

Likewise he named a favourite pool of mine on another river, Hammond's Hideaway, because once there, I never wanted to come away from it. And in this way he catalogued pools and stretches of rivers and gave them names known amongst us all.

Conscious that I might have made this trout stream seem too idyllic by far, and our Boxing Day rituals there seem too summery by far, I can think of no better way of ending this chapter than by quoting what John wrote of the Boxing Day ritual when the heavens opened. Not the previously referred to Boxing Day when the heavens opened, but another one yet again, when the same thing happened. This time there were only four of us mad enough to go out on such a day. This, too, is from John Parsons' *Parsons' Passion*:

> According to Bill, Boxing Day must be observed at least as much for its festive solemnity as for its angling ritual. Freely translated, this means going lightheartedly through the motions of flyfishing as a prelude to lightheartedly downing white wine and fruit-mince pies. We managed the lighthearted second act of our two-act play very creditably today, all things considered. Bolstered by a bottle of champagne topped off with two bottles of wine, the four of us succeeded in presenting an appearance of good cheer.
>
> While Bill and Bryn, sitting in chest waders at the tail of Bill's wagon, dabbled their feet in an ankle-deep muddy puddle, Brian and I sheltered in the back of his wagon, which was parked within a bottle-length of Bill's.
>
> Rain swept down in great pelting curtains from the north-west. It had battered us all morning. Waipunga fishing had never been so wet and so miserable. On arrival, once parked, I knew that if the rain worsened, we had at most three hours to get

out of the valley. One badly washed-out section of the track proved tricky enough coming in. With no tow-rope, the four-wheel-drive couldn't have pulled the other wagon out if necessary on the way back.

Brian and I stuck it for an hour and a half, fighting the incessant wind and rain that hammered at us. At least he hooked a fish. I hooked grass and toitoi heads.

Surface debris sped downstream, and yet the river itself remained eminently fishable. It wasn't until we'd lunched that I studied the river again and found it turning brown.

So we trudged wetly back to the car, expecting to jeer at the other two for having thrown in the towel even faster than we had. Perhaps they would already be observing the second stage of the Boxing Day ritual?

But no. We must have chatted in the car for a good hour before they appeared, grinning, along the track. Bill carried a fine brown trout of 2.5kg. I couldn't believe it. Having landed a brown, Bill had kept it? What next?

Bryn, his face beaming and streaming, explained the phenomenon. The fish had taken the nymph so far down into its throat that they'd had to cut the tippet, but when they'd come to release the fish they'd found it was bleeding. Sadly, Bill killed it.

Inside 10 minutes, with thoughts of lunch ahead to spur his driving virtuosity, Bill was turning the car round to follow ours. If he got stuck, despite the shovels we carried, at least Brian and I in the four-wheel drive could get out of the valley and borrow a tow-rope.

But he made it, and a few minutes later Bryn was pouring champagne. At that magic moment, with the rain nevertheless watering-down the ambrosia

in our raised glasses, the day began to brighten.

Such were our fishing days on that river of magic. Of blessed memories.

LAKE BRUNNER:
THE ORANGIPUKI STREAM

When floating Clouds their spongy Fleeces drain,
Troubling the Streams with swift- descending Rain,
And Waters, tumbling down the Mountain's side,
Bear the loose Soil into the swelling Tide; Then,
soon as Vernal Gales begin to rise, And drive the liq-
uid Burthen through the Skies, The Fisher strait his
Taper Rod prepares, And to the neighbouring
Stream in haste repairs . .

John Gay, *Rural Sports*

LAKE BRUNNER (Westland County, Westland
Province) – A post town thirty-nine miles from
Hokitika, on the road to Christchurch, six or seven
miles from Lake Brunner, and with only small scattered quartz reefs worked in the neighbourhood.
Lake Brunner is a fine sheet of water, popular for
excursions.

Brett's Handy Guide to New Zealand, 1890.

The trouble about combining fishing and touring as part of
a single holiday is that it tends to turn what Zane Grey
used   to call 'expeditions' into becoming mere 'excursions'.
When one needs to condense day-by-day happenings in order
to reach such-and-such a place by sundown to look for a suit-

able hotel or motel it further tends to put pressure on the peripatetic fly fisherman not to waste a single hour of all too precious fishing time, before moving on somewhere else.

On the day my wife and I left Greymouth on the west coast of New Zealand's South Island we were at first undecided whether to consider staying overnight at Mitchells on the shores of nearby Lake Brunner, or to press on by afternoon for Hokitika, further south. My inclination was to stay at Mitchells for perhaps a couple of days; my wife's to move on. The trouble was that it had not stopped raining for several days and nights – at Greymouth the Grey River was about to flood through the town; a reason for hastening our early morning departure – and as we drove inland towards Lake Brunner it seemed even wetter. It was like entering a cold rain forest. A cold, wet, rain forest.

The hotel at Mitchells did nothing to give my wife thoughts of lingering on thereabouts, so I knew that if I wanted to go fishing that day it had to be there and then, despite the fact that the rain fell with the heaviness and never-endingness of the wet monsoon. Some distance on, we parked near the track leading down to the delta of the Orangipuki River where it entered the lake. It lies in a surprising valley between two grassy hills. Even on that first ever visit it seemed like the real New Zealand native bush personified. It seemed older than time, ancient, and quite unchanged by time. Nothing, it seemed, had changed since the land first warmed again after the last of the Ice Ages. The native bush was primeval and exceedingly wet.

Not to be put off, despite the torrential rain, I donned waders and parka, took my fly rod, and hastened through the bush track; not knowing at all exactly where I was going; in fact heading almost instinctively towards the hidden stream. There was not another car for miles around, and certainly no other fishermen. Only fishing fools, such as I most incorrigibly am, would have ventured forth on such a day. They probably had more sense.

The season went by the name of late summer, but it was no more than a figure of speech, as it were. But it was the utter wetness rather than the cold that gave the place a very special and singular atmosphere. It wasn't just wet. It was sodden. Everything was sodden. It wasn't simply rain that fell down through the dark green canopy of native bush, but that it leaked out from everything and everyplace. It did not simply run down the trunks and branches and foliage of the ancient beech trees and primeval tree ferns and pongas: the water simply oozed and squelched out of everywhere; from overhead and underfoot.

There was a clearly defined track through the bush, on either side of which and sheltered by the high canopy of beech and tree ferns grew a dense profusion of the smaller ground ferns. Then unexpectedly, the ferns gave way to raupo and flax. I knew I was close to the stream.

Then I heard the sound of it: the sound of chortling, swirling, running water, on its unhurried but determined way to somewhere else. There was a gap between tall overhanging flax bushes, and the stream seeped up between them. I slipped into the shallow bay, only ankle deep, then out into the main body of the little stream. It was like stepping into a world long ago; like stepping into a picture book; like stepping into a dream.

Great storm clouds rolled in from the west. The sky was a dark palette of ragged nimbus cloud racing along under the towering masses of cumulonimbus. Temporarily, as it turned out, the rain had eased back to a steady downpour, and I was sheltered by the great flax so that it somehow gave the illusion of improvement in the day. The wind blew in sharp gusts, straight in off the lake, no more than a hundred feet out from where I stood. The wind blew against the stream, piling it up in short frothy peaks that seemed to dance up and down in the pewtery light rather than move laterally one way or the other. Wind and current were equal and opposite forces. The stream water had the look of old railway coffee, weakly and badly made, gone cold. Far from indicative of any sort of fishing, my first inclination was to go back to the car with its warmth and dryness.

With no high hopes of expectancy – more in fact to go through the motions of fishing as a sort of ritual – I pulled off some line, then cast out a lightly weighted hare's ear nymph across the stream. It went into the water with a decided plop. I fanned a dozen casts around and about in a near semicircle, then moved downstream a few yards, a little closer to the lake. On the first cast out across the stream the nymph was intercepted in its line of drift, then sucked in hard and taken with a thump. I would hardly have believed that a trout would have seen it in the colouring water. Then I noticed that the water merely looked grey through the solids in suspension, rather than suffused through the water itself. Looking down at my feet I could see the bottom clearly, and was surprised by how well I could see the fish out there at the end of my line.

I beached the fish in the little bay between the flax bushes: a nice hen brown of something over two pounds with flanks the colour of butter and large encircled spots. I prepared to cast out again, this time with more hope than ritual, then sighted a kotuku, the great white heron, standing erect on a ponga stump where the stream entered the lake, looking at me looking at him. And even while I looked and marvelled at this great white bird, supremely regal in its stance and bearing, a pair of blue duck paddled down the centre of the stream.

I felt so much an intruder that I quietly moved away, down to the lake, keeping away from the water, approaching the outlet from the fringe of the lake. My intention was to have a few casts there, then perhaps explore along the lakeshore to investigate whether other outlet streams were nearby.

It only took a few casts up into the stream mouth to hook into the second fish; a slightly larger brown trout this time; once more a hen and golden flanked. I had to net this fish and, as I did so, the white heron took off from its ponga watchtower. I was surprised by the great wingspan and the slow and rhythmic beating of its wings. As it flew by, gaining height, disturbed no doubt by the efforts of my fish to free itself and now recognising me for what I was — an interloping predator of fish — it turned its long white neck in my direction and uttered its characteristic cry, really a croak, for all the world like an angry frog.

Within an hour I had caught and released two more golden flanked brown trout. By now the steadier, constant downpour of rain had altered. It now consisted of torrential squalls, flurrying the lake and stream more wildly, with little spells of relative calms between them, seeming to promise the hope of better, finer weather to come, whereas it steadily got fouler

I had done what I'd set out to do in going fishing, and knew it was time to go back to the car, squelching through the wet, and to drive on towards Hokitika and the far south, and more fishing almost everywhere I went.

As always, I had my ritualistic last three casts for luck, with always another, extra, one single cast – for me. As my fly line curved across the lowering sky I saw the kotuku back on his ponga perch out in the lake shallows. The blue ducks went scuttling by – always surprisingly fast – but quite untroubled by my presence.

I called across the water and wished the great white heron good fishing, then went on my way, wet but well contented.

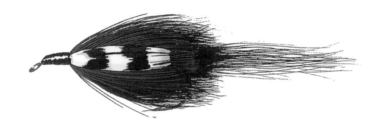

WAIKAREMOANA I
RAINBOWS FROM TANIWHA'S
HAIR

To the Maori of old, the mist-wreathed hills and
valleys held spirits and gods, and even now some
strange presence seems to linger. Man, mountain,
and myth are blended together. Revered ancestors
are not just part of a genealogy but part of the land.
The name of every river and hill, every rock and
tree, brings the history of a thousand years to life
again.

*Land of the Mist – The Story of Urewera National
Park ,* New Zealand Department of Lands &
Survey

This was to be my first visit to Lake Waikaremoana, the
jewel of the Urewera National Park, deep in the remote
mountain fastness of the North Island of New Zealand, the
land of the Tuhoe, the People of the Mist. My first approach
to this great, secret, brooding, but unbelievably   beautiful
place, was by road from Napier, with my friend Alan Bowes
as my guide and mentor.

The road from Napier to Wairoa is a good one, but that is
only part of the journey towards one of the only two roads into
the Urewera. Soon after Frasertown down in the   pastoral

Waiau River valley the tortuous upward climb begins. An American writer once described a fishing camp he had visited in New Zealand as being at the very end of the very worst road in all the world. Now it may have seemed like it to him, but I happen to know that road well; the one into the Waimana River through Taneatua, which compared to either of the two roads into Waikaremoana is a mere and gentle doddle.

Many such back country roads are of pure pumice: one day they can be graded, flat and easy going, with not too many pot holes or slips at their outer edges; while the next day, after rain, they can be deeply rutted, transversely corrugated from run-offs, and anything from heavy, tortuous, slow-going to utterly impassable. Both roads into Waikaremoana – the Te Whaiti-Ruatahuna road in from Murupara to the northwest, or the steep climb in through Rangiahua and Tuai to the southeast – are of different mettle and of bone-shuddering construction. They have been hewn out from solid rock. On good days the tennis-ball-size but jagged boulders lie in what seems an orderly manner; more or less flat-surfaced, with only a lane of deep ruts gouged out by the daily Railways Bus. On bad days, however, the shingle will be piled high, especially on corners, of which there are many, with all the trickery and danger for an unwise motorist of treacherous shifting sands. The road, in fact, is a shifting sands and a desert of tennis ball size hewn stone. But while they shift and slide under the stress of a passing car, they have none of that saving plasticity of the unmetalled pumice road. There are times, too, when the ruts between the metal are deep enough to entrap the wheels of a car, yet not broad enough at their peaks to drive above them.

The road we took on that, my first trip in, was such a road, and in those days it was ten times as bad as it is today. Steadily, we climbed up ever higher along the twisting, winding, circuitous road that for the most part follows the even steeper descent of the Waikaretaheke River. Hereabouts the country is wild and savage. Even without knowing anything about the mythology and legends of the place it is impossible not to sense a palpable awareness that this tortured road leads upwards into a secret country quite cut off from the lush pastoral world below, through which we had only so recently driven. There is an almost overpowering awareness of climbing up into another world.

Alan, being the man he is, stopped a few times along the steep ascent to brew sweet hot tea from streamwater boiled in the Volcano. Standing there, looking down and outwards as far as the eye could see across this twisted convoluted landscape, as if in another world, the strong tea took on the taste of a hitherto unknown, untasted nectar, although that other world – almost the floating world of Japan – lay still several hundred feet upwards and many miles onwards.

It was a day in early December. Despite the calendar seasonal approach to midsummer there was still only a hint of it in the air. There was still a distinct chill in the breeze; only a sheltered, full sun had any warmth. Great swathes of towering cumulus cloud rolled by overhead, heading out towards the South Pacific Ocean.

At the time of that first visit I was less steeped in the legends of Waikaremoana than I am today, but had already read much about the place, so that I would not be making the last steep climb past Tuai and Kaitawa up over the lip of the high yet still mountainous plateau encircling Lake Waikaremoana, wholly ignorant of the legends out of which the place itself was created.

The Maori peoples of New Zealand are steeped in their ancient lore and tales of their beginnings. Like their aboriginal counterparts in Australia, and the American Indians of the United States and Canada, the Maori were animists in believing that all natural objects are inhabited by spirits, and that they themselves have sprung from this same well of being. Much to the detriment of the European's understanding of such peoples, the very nature of our culture has not only denied, but ridiculed, such beliefs. Paradoxically, it is now

114

through the mathematics of quantum mechanics and a new understanding of the nature of ultimate reality, that we are being led towards a glimmer of understanding what these supposedly primitive peoples have been trying to tell us all along – except that we did not listen. It was unfashionable to listen.

Relative to the Australian Aborigine and the North American Indian, who have dwelt in their lands since the Dreaming, the Maori is almost as much a newcomer to New Zealand as the non-indigenous white Pakeha. They came by canoe from the islands of the South Pacific. Their history is told in the spoken poetry by word of mouth, and like much history is twisted in the telling. Paradoxically their myths have almost universal backgrounds. They had no written language, so that everything – their history, their genealogy, their pre-history, their gods and devils, and the story of their creation – needed to be told, again and again, down every generation. Like Islam it became a way of life.

Nothing, no part of it, was separate from anything else. Everything was inextricably linked up in a great flux. In such a society it is pointless to ask where factual remembered truth ends, and only myths and legends extend back further in time. And in case we scoff at such indetermination, as we tend to do, we would do well to remember that even our most recent history is being constantly rewritten and reappraised from one generation to the next at a breathtaking speed. Truth is blurred, to say the least, at its most recent edges.

Our own creation myth was not from the deep wells of our own past, but borrowed from Judaism. The question as to what God did the day before he began creation as we know it does not enter into the Aboriginal or American Indian scheme of things. For them the earth itself first came into being, and in that being was its very essence. It was an empty world, but then the earth spirit multiplied until it inhabited the rocks, the earth, the lakes and rivers. For them, man's totemic ancestors, whether they were fish or fowl or beast came into being out of pure spirit. Then man came and sang the world into being.

By naming things he not only indentified them but gave them actuality.

The Maori of New Zealand arrived in a fleet of canoes from somewhere out in Polynesia. The islands from whence they came were mostly small and simple, and the island spirits came with them, now to a vastly more complex land. Because the Australian Aborigine and the North American Indian had sung the world into existence, they needed to go on singing their wanderings to keep it going, to maintain its equilibrium. In much the same way, many of today's most brilliant physicists actually ponder as to whether or in what sense a tree or a flower or a rock may be said to exist, if there is no one there to see it. Can a sound be said to have any existence if there is no one there to hear it?

Nonsensical as such ideas might be to us, they would have seemed quite ordinary and understandable to the 'primitive' peoples we are talking about – at least before our impinging, invasive culture disoriented them.

The Maori, then, without song in the way we know it, were spirit-haunted people who became great declaimers. The spoken word was everything; as much for them the key to the future as it was to their ancestral past. And in such a manner they were a people who began all their tales as, indeed, until very recent years we ourselves did: Once upon a time was the prelude to the future, to right and proper behaviour, to life, just as much as it was a race memory of the mythical past; things, knowledge, remembered.

I have already mentioned this great and foreboding sense and awareness of entering another world, as it were, in coming to Waikaremoana. This is how Maori legend had the great landscape come into being:

Long ago there lived a very great chief named Maahu-tapoa-nui. He lived with his wife Kau-ariki at Waikotikoti, now known as Wairaumoana. At this time there was no great lake, but below Panekiri lay a deep valley where many tributary streams flowed into an ancient river.

One evening Maahu called to his daughter Hau-mapuhia to fetch him some water from Te Puna-a-taupara, the sacred well. But Hau-mapuhia would not go, and her father flew into a rage at her disrespect. She told him that if he wanted water from the well he could fetch it himself. In a murderous fury Maahu took the calabash and went to the well. There he quenched his thirst but not his raging anger. He waited by the well until Hau-mapuhia was sorry and came to find her father.

At last she came, but by now Maahu's anger knew no bounds and he seized Hau-mapuhia and thrust her head under the stream waters. Hau-mapuhia had no chance against her father's power and she began to drown. In a desperate bid to escape she cried out to the gods of the land. They heeded her pleas and as she died her human form became a powerful tani-wha – a water monster – and twisted out of Maahu's grasp, thrashing the earth this way and that.

Hau-mapuhia knew that as a taniwha the light of day would cause her death, even as a taniwha, and she struggled to force her way to the safety of the ocean. First she thrust northwards but her way was barred by the Huiarau Range, and to this day we see the gouge she made as the Whanganui arm of the lake. In a panic she tore at the earth, making great channels and hollows where the water rushed in to form further arms and inlets until the familiar star-shaped lake we know today was created by the titanic upheavals of her spreadeagled body, face downwards in the deep waters.

Her last attempt was to escape at Te Wharawhara, the outlet of the lake near Onepoto. She forced her way through the narrow barrier at this point, but as she emerged, head down at Whangaromanga, the dawn spread across the waters.

As the first rays of the sun slanted through the sky, she made a last anguished movement towards the sea, but it was too late. The dawn light found her face down, turned to stone. There she still lies, and the waters of the lake flow through her petrified body. Sometimes jets of water would rise in the air above her, or her voice would wail in the wind, and men would fear a great storm on the lake.

And now, even to this day, at Onepoto we can look down into the crystal clear water and see her hair, in the more prosaic form of a kelp-like fresh water plant called kohuwai, floating, waving and weaving in undulating tresses deep down in the waters of the lake. Only the taniwha's hair has movement and life. The rest of her lies petrified, turned to stone, while the great jagged boulders of rock lying everywhere at the lake outlet are the lasting evidence of her titanic struggles to reach the outer ocean and eternity.

To the Maori of old, the mist-wreathed hills and valleys held spirits and gods, and even now some strange presence seems to linger. Man, mountain, lake, and myth are blended together. Revered ancestors are not just part of a genealogy, but part of the land. The name of every river and hill, every rock and tree, brings the history of a thousand years to life and immediate significance.

On a more mundane level the geological record shows that Lake Waikaremoana was formed by a massive natural landslide which dammed the Waikaretaheke River. Forested valleys were flooded, and many of the drowned trees remain as standing stumps on the lakebed. At other places around the lakeshore there are outcrops of petrified trees, turned into stone like the taniwha herself.

This gigantic natural dam at Onepoto remained for countless centuries the lake's one outlet. Most of the outflow was through subsurface leaks seeping through the giant boulders, but when the lake level was high it would have flowed out over Onepoto in a gigantic waterfall. A remarkable feature of Waikaremoana, and especially of the outlet arm at Onepoto, lies in the extraordinary clarity of the lake water, permitting rooted aquatic plants down to depths of more than sixty feet to be seen as if they were no more than six feet down. Hence Taniwha's Hair.

So there we were that day, Alan Bowes and myself, driving up the steep and winding road from Tuai and Kaitawa to Lake Waikaremoana – the perfect name for it: The Sea of Sparkling Waters. High above us, at that point in our steep ascent, more recently than the time of the taniwha's mythological adventures – as recently, in fact, as 1946, twin tunnels had been driven through the natural dam created in some primeval landslide so that water could flow through huge penstocks to Kaitawa Power Station. From there the water passed through the small Lake Kaitawa, then downwards on through further penstocks to drive the power station on Lake Whakamarino at Tuai.

When this was done it created a new and sardonic twist in the life cycles of the local races of acclimatized brown and rainbow trout. Lake Waikaremoana, high above, almost 2000 feet above sea level, extends in its star-shaped spread about a shoreline of some sixty miles and a depth of over 800 feet. Lake Kaitawa, four hundred feet below, is a small water; while Lake Whakamarino, yet another 600 feet still lower, is a little larger, extending about half a mile across.

Way up above, in Waikaremoana itself, trout often congregate in the narrowing waters of the outlet arm where drifting food organisms are funnelled in towards them. But when the drift is strongest, the penstocks are open and many an unwary trout is sucked into these gigantic tubular waterways and dispatched down through the droning turbines below; then on again, down through Tuai into Lake Whakamarino, where another tribe of related huge brown and rainbow trout wax fat on a regular diet of minced trout from their unlucky brethren above. Whakamarino has thus become a trophy water of sorts for a certain type of New Zealand trout fisherman. Twenty-pounders are fairly commonplace. Quite recently a brown trout of more than 27 pounds was taken from this small water. Needless to say, not every fly fisherman's idea of fishing heaven.

And still less needless to say, not on our list of fishing places on that first day as we climbed up over the steep hill on our way to the pristine waters of Lake Waikaremoana itself.

In all probability I did not dwell upon or even think about the legend of Hau-mapuhia drowned and changed into being a Taniwha – a water monster – up there in the waters of the lake we were coming to fish. At least not on the journey. I was already familiar with the tale, but had read about it with that detachment with which one usually first reads a mytho-logical story. I had as yet attached no sense of place to the myth.

I was aware, too, that one of the first Europeans to pene-trate into the Ureweras, the Rev. J. G. Laughton, had stood on the brow of the natural dam at Onepoto, looking out over the country up and over which we had travelled, and wrote of it: ' . . . range beyond range stretching . . . to the horizon, a fan-tastic green sea sweeping southwestwards from the Pacific.' I remembered, too, what Katherine Mansfield said of it when she journeyed through Urewera early this century: 'it is all so gigantic and tragic – and even in the bright sunlight it is so passionately secret.'

It was Alan's intention that we should fish at Onepoto first, before driving on around the lake to the old Government-owned fishermen's huts below the Lake House, where we were to stay. We came through the topmost cutting on the crown of the hill, then down towards Onepoto. Across the bay and out towards the main body of the lake lies the com-manding Panekire Bluff, rising almost sheer two thousand feet above the lake surface.

The first sight of this often dark and mysterious corner of the lake at this point does not overwhelm the senses with utter beauty, or of the picturesque, as does the main body of the lake itself. It looks for all the world like an up-ended Giant's Causeway: as if these hundreds of thousands of oddly squared-off rocks, as big as ten or more foot cubes, have been placed there by some unnatural agency, as if they were tum-bled straight out of heaven.

And there they lie today, difficult to negotiate, leading fairly steeply to the waters of the lake, yet in some places seeming more like rising terraces of breakwaters against the sea. The bedrock of the narrow bay consists of banded sandstone and siltstone weathered down through ages to a series of projecting sills of the harder, more durable sandstone.

We set up our fly rods and made our way down towards the water. No foreshore anywhere here: just giant blocks of rock leading straight into deep water, terraced like some megalithic amphitheatre. On first approach the water looks almost dark and unfathomable, but this is a strange illusion about the place that in no way changed in many subsequent visits spread out over several years, seasons, and times of day. Another strange thing about Onepoto is that it always seems cold down there close by the water.

I had on a fast sinking line, a Hamill's Killer, and I cast out for the very first time over the Sea of Sparkling Waters. At first glance, there seemed nothing sparkling about this particular dark end of the big lake. A diffused sunlight spread out from somewhere behind me, but the sun itself was low behind a range of mountains. It seemed as if the natural lighting down there in this rugged valleyed outlet channel – for it was just as steep on the other side, where Alan had crossed over to fish.

My fly line hissed out over the darkly rippling water. I watched the line hug at first in the surface tension, then slice downwards through the water in a beautiful curve. My first reaction was to think that the fly line was sinking very slowly, which puzzled me. Then I realised that it was, in fact, hurtling down into the depths – but that I was mesmerised. Far from being darkly turbid, as I had first thought, I saw that the water was of extraordinary clarity. I could see the fly line to its far extremity, until it dangled there, almost up and down, and I felt certain that fly line and fly would certainly foul in some jagged rocks on the retrieve.

But when I began the retrieve I observed something else;

quite strange, as if outside the natural law. I could see the fly
line going almost straight down into the depths, close against
this fantastic wall of almost vertical rocks. But as I retrieved I
saw the lower section of the fly line billow outwards away
from the rockface, as if it was being wafted out by a submarine current. Then I began to make out – possibly because
rapidly shifting clouds were throwing different shadow patterns on the water – that what I had assumed were vague and
distorted images of rocks on the bottom were no such thing.
The bottom was far more profound. The shimmering, wafting,
fleeting shadows I had mistakenly taken for the lakebed were
upright upward growing fronds of a darkly brown kelp-like
plant. It was this broad-leafed shimmering vegetation down
there that gave the water an illusory opacity. It was crystal
clear. I was fishing in Taniwha's hair.

Equally remarkable as never snagging the submerged rocks
on the face of the downward slope, was that I never seemed to
snag any of the wafting underwater fronds. It was as if the fly
was guided by magic: and especially so as I was the driver
because, in every other water I've ever fished, I am the champion snagger and can hook up into a tree or a bending toitoi,
or even a single stalk of tough grass, with certain ease. Here
in Taniwha's hair my artificial fly was guided as if by magic.

Cast after cast there was a mesmeric repetition in sending
out the line again and again across the water, and in the fasci-
nation I subsequently had in watching the jerkily tweaked
ascent of my fly through the underwater trailing fronds of
kohuwai. Suddenly, I was awakened out of this trance-like
state by the screech of the reel and the high leaping of a
hooked trout and the bend of Alan's rod on the other side.
Soon afterwards I saw him net the fish, and in the next quarter hour or so he hooked and lost another two, but landed one
other.

Meanwhile, I was still trying to grow accustomed to the
strange magic of the place. It had – at least for me – a feel to
it quite impossible to describe, but undeniably real. It was not

spookily eery, but it did seem to radiate a sense of uncanny presence. Then, it seemed strangely cold; but not cold in any disturbing way. This was merely a marker of its difference. Then, too, there was a distinctive but quite unnatural sound of wind as if soughing through trees – yet there were no trees thereabouts and, by the patterns of wavelets on the water, not wind enough to sigh, let alone sough. Yet, without doubt, there was a faint but fairly consistent murmuring sound; no doubt caused by the somewhat confined and soundbowl shape of the outlet itself, and having nothing to do with the petrified Taniwha forever sleeping on the lakebed.

Although lulled by the repetitive rhythms of casting and retrieve I was still fishing with a sense of heightened aware-ness. Indeed, it is only because I felt that way, so many years ago now, that I can still remember with such startling clarity exactly how it was that day. Since then I have had – and enjoyed – perhaps hundreds of fishing occasions about which I have long since forgotten everything, as if they had never happened.

The cast that mattered most was the one when the sun came over the mountain peak behind me. Suddenly, the outlet reach of the lake was bathed in a golden glow, as if amber floodlights had been switched on. The deep current that bore fly line and fly out and away from the steep underwater drop-off, sudden-ly seemed even more effective, so that the retrieved fly swam upwards in a curving arc through the now sometimes golden, sometimes sea-green tresses of Taniwha's hair, undulating down there in the deep water.

And as the fly itself swam into sight I watched the diaphanous but certain shape and form of a rainbow trout streaking upwards after it. My Hamill's Killer was engulfed, and the fish turned back downwards into the depths, back through the long tresses of Taniwha's hair. Soundly hooked, the trout bore downwards. My rod tip bent over in a doubling semicircle of delight. The reel shrieked and blotted out the unknown murmurings in the air. The line streaked off the reel, disappearing into the depths of the lake. Then the fly line was all out beyond the rod tip, and the backing played a different tune on the reel drum, quieter, but harsher; less music to my ears. Then I watched the outstretched line cut through the water like a sharp fin. I could feel the deep-bellying fly line cutting through the strangely upward, light-seeking fronds of kohuwai, but slipping, sliding through them with ease and no restriction. Then up came the fish in a vertical climb out of the water fifty yards out, perhaps more, in a great cascade of showering sparkling water. But I was nowhere in touch with the trout and stripped in line frantically in a wild effort to make contact again with that other world.

Suddenly, there was a run towards the open lake, away to my right, and as the line ran out from around my feet I prayed it would not foul the rocks, or even foul up upon itself in some hopeless tangle. I was able to guide it out until the full weight of the running fish was happily taken up by my rod and reel and line.

Soon afterwards I shortened up and withdrew upwards through the shimmering tresses of Taniwha's hair my first Waikaremoana rainbow trout. Netted and weighed, she proved to be a female fish, like Taniwha herself, but no mythological monster this: instead a lovely rainbow of just a shade over four pounds.

My love affair with Waikaremoana had begun.

WAIKAREMOANA II
INTO THE LAND OF THE
MIST

> . . . the valley – the air – the shining water . . . at
> the head of a great valley the blazing sun uplifts
> itself – like a gigantic torch to light the bush – it is
> all so gigantic and tragic – and even in the bright
> sunlight it is so passionately secret . . . We begin to
> reach the valley – broad and green – red and brown
> butterflies – the green place in vivid sunlight and
> the silent and green bush – The sunlight slanting in
> to the trees – an island – then a river arched with
> tree fern – And always through the bush the hushed
> sound of water running on brown pebbles – It seems
> to breathe the full deep bygone essence of it all – a
> fairy formation of golden rings . . .
>> **Katherine Mansfield, *The Urewera Notebook***

The first visits I made to Lake Waikaremoana were by road,
in from Napier and Wairoa on the east coast. It was only
after I had gone to live at Taupo that I made the journey into
the Ureweras through the only other way in, the road from
Murupara in the west. Despite certain superficial characteristics in the characters of the two inroads – the chief of which
they were both awful, although this I found, over the years,

was a blessing of sorts because the sheer awfulness of the roads in was so daunting, it kept most would-be visitors away, and was the only real preserver of the wilderness – but despite this common barrier they shared in about equal proportions, the two roads into Waikaremoana were so different and passed through such different country, it seemed that each one was leading into two entirely different worlds.

Arriving from the Wairoa, eastern end, the visitor at first had no sense of being in a National Park and, albeit that the landscape was of grandeur, it was in no way sublime. Up, over the crest of the outlet landslide, and one was there, right beside the fantastically beautiful lake. The lake itself dominates everything from such an arrival. The road from Onepoto skirts close by the lakeshore; sometimes almost alongside sunlit sandy bays; at others winding, twisting through a road blasted out from the solid rock of a cliff high above the lake, where one's sight of this sea of sparkling waters is as if from the sky.

In startling contrast the road in through Murupara is almost straight into the Land of the Mist, a different world from that of the Sea of Sparkling Waters, albeit again, that both roads meet face to face, and one becomes the other, heading back towards the places one has recently passed through. And this junction of the two worlds is not at all that inappropriately placed at the National Park Headquarters at Aniwaniwa on the northeastern arm of the lake.

Looking back on it now, after several years, I feel glad that on my first visit to the lake via the Murupara road I stopped to go fishing where some vaguely understood sense directed me to go before continuing on around the lakeshore to the Park Headquarters.

Murupara is a typical small logging town on the eastern boundary of the Kaingaroa Forest. The wide alluvial plain of the Rangitaiki River valley suitably cuts off the new exotic forest of fast-growing pines from the rugged bush-clad peaks of the Ikawhenua Range that leads into the secret mountain fastness off Urewera. Murupara boasts a few pubs and stores and other trappings of civilisation but, sadly, the younger generations of Maori people seem to spend most of their days sitting around the town square, seeming as if somewhere along their path they have somehow lost their way. But just a mile or so outside the small town the little groups of houses suddenly come to an end. The road bears steeply, tortuously up into the ranges. It winds through dense native bush; the road itself a hewn-out track metalled with loose stone aggregate possessing all the fluid attributes, but none of the softness, of shifting sands. Stones lie piled deeper than axle high on either side, and almost as high in the middle. The only way through it is to drive on in the previous vehicle's ruts. It is a bone-shaking experience at best. At its worst the road is impassable.

Along the way one passes ancient Maori settlements: Te Whaiti, Ngaputahi, Heipipi, and on to Ruatahuna, ever climbing over the great ranges. Here there are few cars, but horses almost everywhere. The people suddenly look different. These are not town Maori: they have long, dark features; there is something un-Polynesian about them. They have the strangely surprising look of some ancient forgotten semitic tribe. They are a secret looking people, with secret-looking faces, and even if one stops at the store in Ruatahuna to buy some snack for the journey, one is served curtly and dismissively and made to feel a stranger, a foreigner, an interloper in their land. These are Tuhoe, the first people of Urewera. Among all other Maori tribes they are 'the Children of the Mist'. Many assume this name of the Urewera tribe derives from the mists that ever wreathe the forest peaks of their land, but the derivation is from their mythological dreaming. In this creation myth the Tuhoe are descendants from the marriage of Hine-pukohu-rangi, the goddess, the celestial Mist Maiden, with the sacred mountain, Maunga-pohatu. Even among the declamatory genealogies of the lowland Maori tribes they interpret this to mean that there is no way to discover how long the original people lived in the Ureweras – it is lost in the mists of time. The Tuhoe may stem from forefathers already settled hereabouts in New Zealand long before the first canoe fleet arrived from the Maori traditional home island of Hawaiiki.

When a Tuhoe looks at one, straight in the eye, impassively, seeing everything but giving away nothing, only the most insensitive Pakeha can feel anything but a gross, insufferable intruder. And the dark look is unforgettable. At Ruatahuna we have already entered a new and different world, but are still only halfway along the winding road that leads to Waikaremoana. From here on the road cuts through true wilderness.

Even if the day is fine and there are the wispy high cirrus clouds of fine weather, wreaths of mist can be seen almost everywhere around: from high on the peaks, to swirling mere tree-top high as one gazes down into a jagged bush-clad valley beneath the winding, climbing road. At best there will be wisps of mist everywhere. At its worst, the entire landscape can seem encased, enshrouded in a carpeting of swirling mist. The air is cold and clean, but must have the wettest smell of air on earth. On a good day, in high summer, the convoluted landscape virtually steams.

The landforms throughout the entire National Park area are stable and enduring. But on this western part of the Ureweras layers of ash and pumice from ages past volcanic activity, around Taupo and Rotorua, still cover the ancient bedrock. The great stands of natural forest so characteristic of Waikaremoana are noticeably stratified with altitude. The more lowland forests are distinctive with large round-headed rata and rimu rising above dense stands of tawa and tawhero trees. As the road climbs through the forest, tawa becomes more abundant, together with large miro. Higher still red and silver beech reach up and cover the highest ranges.

The branches and foliage of the larger trees form a canopy, a close and tight knit layer screening out most direct sunlight from the forest interior. But the greatest of the trees emerge above and through the canopy. Far beneath, shaded by the great canopy grow the giant tree ferns and lianes, and beneath them yet again the smaller ferns, all in wild profusion.

The forest is alive with birds, but except for the native pigeon, kereru, and the fantail, waxeye, bellbird, and tui, most other birds – the kaka, being one – are most likely to be heard, but rarely seen.

Even driving through this forest on our way into Waikaremoana the place is awe inspiring. It is easy to understand how the Maori saw nature in a spiritual sense. Indeed, it is impossible to contemplate that it could be seen in any other way, and makes one aware that it is we who are the losers on account of having made a holy grail of materialistic progress.

Rivers and streams abound almost everywhere. In such wild country mountains and valleys follow no pastoral orderliness or pattern, so that springs and streams may source from any conceivable nook and cranny. Mountain becks become rivers in a single mile and may tumble over some great waterfall hundreds of feet below as tributary to a fast-growing river. Often crossing and criss-crossing such streams it seems there is no logic in direction of flow. A stream might run due north for awhile, then spill over a great scarp to augment another altogether different stream heading south . Water is everywhere.

The road in from Ruatahuna reaches the far northern shores of Lake Waikaremoana at the Whanganui Inlet. We drove right in to the high ridge overlooking the Hopuruahine Landing. Here the Rahuiatemata Stream widens out into a sluggishly uncharacteristic flow into the lake, but the apparently easy-moving body of water belies the upstream mass of it that pours, only a mile upstream, through and over the Takapou-O-Hinewai Cascades as the Hopuruahine Stream tumbles out of the mountainside towards the nearby lake.

The Hopuruahine Cascades was to be our first stop, but

first we looked down from high above into the narrowing reach not far upstream from the Landing. There were armies of trout marshalling down there below us. Mostly they finned the current, holding seemingly choreographed stations in groups of three or four. Then, suddenly, from the outer shallower curve of the farside bank slightly lesser trout would attempt to move in at speed, as if to drive out the resident holders of the deeper holding waters. It seemed a sort of dance; perhaps no more than jockeying for position. The air was crystal clear and the stream water below was gin clear, but the size of the trout below was eye-popping. Even the 'smallest' of them looked to be four, five, or six pounds apiece; while the more magisterial and solid phalanx of the bigger fish must all have been between ten and twelve pounds in weight, or even more.

At the time of that first visit most New Zealand fly fishermen favoured fishing the rips, where streams flowed into lakes, and almost completely ignored venturing upstream. It was a habit born of custom, but had become so cloaked in a form of dogma it took on the near sanctity of revealed truth. From our high vantage point we could see two anglers fishing the stream mouth, and two anglers at that time, fishing together in one place at any stream mouth around Waikaremoana, constituted a crowd.

Instead of wading upstream from the flats below us, entailing much crossing and re-crossing of often deep and turbulent water as the river climbed and twisted through a steep rise, we decided to head straight up overland to the Hopuruahine Cascades. Once started up the track it was like entering another world. Dense native bush grows in gnarled and twisted shapes, issuing forth from clefts and crannies in the bewildering and overwhelming ravines of giant blocks of tumbled sandstone that make up the course of the upper river.

The song of bellbirds echoed everywhere. Grey warblers darted among the bush. Waxeyes, fantails, and above the lower canopy, wherever there was a clearing with taller trees emerging there would be a lumbering kereru, the native pigeon.

We reached the lower pool where the tumbling mountain stream cascades down through clefts in the ravine, roaring its way down, scintillating spray flying everywhere in a rainbow haze. Right at the head of the deep pool the white water foams out from three directions above, between a spillway of huge tumbled boulders. But even these huge, centuries' water-worn rocks are dwarfed by an enormous flat-topped over-hanging slab of stone that casts a shadow over the still back-water bay worn out by time and the endless flow of swirling water to one side of the main cascade. One look at such a place and even the most insensitive man or woman would know it possessed a very special quality.

Just in front of the giant flat-topped block of stone; itself a primitive megalith carved out by nature and the hardest of all chisels – water itself – stands a smaller rock that provides a natural casting platform in what must surely be one of nature's most incredibly beautiful settings. From this easily mounted rock it is possible to survey and cast into any part of the pool.

To one's left there is a quieter backwater of pale green translucent water, deep, deep, straight down under the giant flat-topped block of stone. As one's eye becomes accustomed to the place it becomes apparent that the relative opacity of this backwater is only because of the complex web of water movement patterns with increasing depth: different levels of water are moving in different directions, so that the effect of looking downwards into its depths creates a shimmering illusion of haziness. I watched a trout down there – deep down – and as it swam downwards, deeper still, through different levels, it seemed as if it had been cut into two pieces, caused by the complex air-bubble filled tricks of refraction and trompe d'oeile. Trout can be hard enough to see deep down in a pool under the most normal conditions, but in this particular back-water corner of the cascade pool they were positively disem-bodied and amorphously ghostlike.

To one side of these shimmering depths, at the very neck of the pool, a rolling sheet of white water curved downwards, plunging perhaps fifteen feet into the foaming waters beneath. A myriad bubble-entrapped blobs of air kaleidoscoped down into the depths, tumbling, rolling, about each other. The surface white water ran hard against the sheer boulders across the pool, then hugged that far bank, leaving the clear waters directly in front of me remarkably untroubled by all this turbulence. It was as if the entire mass of water was visually and hydrodynamically layered, like a cake – but vertically, too. A straightish line of foam extended below to the tail of the pool, where the fast flowing waters tumbled out again. And deep down under the outer flecks of white foam I could make out the clear shapes of large trout moving in and out under the shadow of the heavy white surface water. They looked like animated submarines.

New Zealand is doubly blessed with such places and such fishing, yet the two have not always gone together. The Hopuruahine Cascades were there way back in the mists of time, almost since the days when the world was new. But until the coming of the white man as settler in the middle years of the last century the stream in front of me, and even the vastness of Lake Waikaremoana itself, held nothing but a sparse and insignificant fauna of fishes. The waters were troutless.

The gigantic landslide at Onepoto that first created the lake from drowned river valleys probably occurred 2200 years ago. Up until then migratory long-finned eels and koaro would have had little difficulty in climbing the steep falls. The indigenous bully and kokopu, the inanga, dwarf galaxias and torrentfish, made up sparse fish populations.

Introductions by man altered all that, with the entry of brown trout in 1896 and rainbow trout in 1907. The trout prospered. In 1948 it was necessary to introduce common smelt to urgently supplement the diet of the trout.

Spawning runs of trout into the tributary streams of Waikaremoana are mostly limited by the ubiquitous presence of steep waterfalls close to the lake itself. The spawning runs are dominated by brown trout. But this does not reflect the true ratio of brown to rainbow trout in the lake, because brown trout are that much longer-lived, their populations have a greater proportion of mature fish. In the lake, the population of rainbow trout comprises mostly immature fish, and these make up the bulk of the average fisherman's catch – especially in that most of the fishing is done by trolling from boats. fly-fishermen fishing from the shore catch mostly brown trout and, later in the season, mature rainbows. It was once estimated that brown trout comprise seventy per cent of the combined trout populations, although rainbow made up eighty-seven per cent of the anglers' catch.

The trout we had seen marshalling in the lower reaches would have been all browns, although there was every chance that bigger than average rainbows would be competing with even bigger browns in the fast white water of the cascades pool.

By the time I made a subsequent visit to the Hopuruahine Falls a few years later, I had learned that a big bushy dry fly – a cicada, in season – cast upstream along the smoother waterline, close and parallel to the line of frothy white water in such a mountain pool would often raise a big trout from out of the depths. But on this first visit neither of us even dreamed of such a practice in such heavy turbulent water; so much false dogma do we pick up along our angling path. Instead, I approached the natural casting platform with a fast sinking line and my favourite (in doubt) Red Setter fly.

It was all trial and error. Cast in one direction, the fly line would belly downstream in a most unnatural manner, dragging the fly round in a sweeping, accelerating arc. For perhaps half an hour or so I cast up and across into foaming water directly under the falls. The line would tighten nicely as it sank and the weight of water came on it, and I envisaged my fly trundling deep in the fast white water directly opposite me on the far side of the pool, fishing well down there before arc-ing in at the tail and ready to be retrieved. Once, twice, I thought I had a strong pull, but they would have been hard to detect in the heavy water, so I didn't pay too much store by these little bursts of adrenalin.

In casting more directly up into the head of the pool, I could see the uncontrolled snaking loops of fly line as it sank through the clear sunlit water. It didn't seem a likely productive line of casting, because I was never in real tactile contact with the fly. But at least it made a change in the limited range of casts available to me, so I included a few such in the probing, semi-circular tour of casts I made into this utterly enchanting water.

Then, in one such cast, when in my mind I had an idea that my deep-sunk fly was still up the pool somewhere in front of me, there was an explosion in the fast white water away to my right, towards the far side of the pool. It was a fish all right, tail-walking up towards the falls. I still didn't connect that it had anything to do with me, until the fly line whizzed out through my fingers and my fly rod bent over in a vibrant arc.

With great good fortune I soon had firm line and hand contact with the trout: now boring deep into the depths of the pool, with that savage tugging and headshaking so characteristic of a good fish that plans to make its escape and seems to know how best to do it. It was an up, down struggle for the most part, relieved at times by the most deliberate and persistent motoring around the perimeter of the pool, but always deep down.

But the hard, fast water down there was doing its work for me and the trout was beginning to ebb. I was able to rock-hop some distance downstream towards the next cascade – there was nowhere else to go, no other place of hope – and by dint of the most injudicious sidestrain hold the trout close up against the face of a rocky bay where the water slackened. More by luck than judgement, I later realised , I held out my landing net and slid rather than guided the trout into it. It was a brown of five pounds – a handsome jack – not, admittedly one of the giants observed downstream, but a fine fish all the same, and a perfect outcome for this my first visit to a new place.

From there I scrambled down to the lower pool in time to watch J. C-P. land a six-pound brown. But where did the giants of their tribe go once into this short stretch of river? There was certainly no time to investigate the matter just then. The afternoon shadows were lengthening and the sun no longer penetrated down to us in the cascades. It was time to move on down the lake to Home Bay where we had booked a cabin, at that time the only visitor accommodation available.

We drove on around the lakeshore. As we went past the Mokau Falls the last rays of the weakening sun flooded across the inlet and transformed the great waterfall into a shimmering golden veil.

Four days of glorious fishing lay ahead. This was but a start to it.

WAIKAREMOANA III
THE LAKE IN THE CLOUDS

. . . The next morning sees us ferried across the head of the inlet and landed on the right bank of the creek, from which spot a two-hours' walk up the range brings us to Waikareiti. On reaching the top of the hill, we descend a small spur for a short distance, and see through the trees before us the calm, silent waters of Waikareiti. This beautiful lake is surrounded by low hills covered with dense forest, which extends to the water's edge, the branches trailing in the water in many places. There are none of the great cliffs and ranges of the larger lake here; the scenery is not grand, as is that of Waikaremoana, but it is nevertheless very beautiful, there being many little islands in the lake, all densely clothed with bush. One longs for a canoe at canoeless Waikareiti to go out, and explore those lonely islets, and paddle across the shining waters.
Elsdon Best, Waikaremoana *The Sea of Rippling Waters: The Lake; The Land; The Legends with A Tramp Through Tuhoe Land 1897*

. . . A weird and silent place is Waikare- iti, with its unexplored isles and great forest; a most beauti-

136

ful and   unknown spot, but bearing no sign of the
presence of   man. Verily the Bohemian spirit longs
to go and explore   those silent islands and search
for traces of ancient   occupation thereon, from the
days when the "children"   of Ruapani and the
ancient Tauira held these lone lands . . .

Elsdon Best, Waikaremoana, 1897.

Waikaremoana is said to be the most beautiful lake in New
Zealand, and other tales in this book have dwelt upon
its utter remoteness and pristine natural beauty. Once there,
at the lake level, two thousand feet above sea level, even the
most unimaginative visitor feels on top of the world, as if he is
among the world's rooftops. Yet the twenty-two square miles
of Lake Waikaremoana itself are surrounded by mountains,
and at the summit of one lies yet another lake that seems to
belong to an entirely different world.

This lake is Waikareiti – meaning Little Rippling Waters –
and it lies at the summit of an ancient beech forest mountain
track after a climb of a further nine hundred feet above
Waikaremoana itself. The climb is steep, but easy going
through yet another world. The ancient beeches appear to be
dwarfed, but this is an illusion caused by the unreliable human
eye being forced to look either acutely upwards or downwards
along the steep incline. Added to this the bush is dense, so that
one rarely sees a great beech tree, standing alone, at any distance.

The panorama is a short scale one; a close up – and, like all
close-ups, what one looks at is foreshortened and somehow
distorted by the sheer majesty of it all, all jumbled together.
The track through the beech forest is through a shaded,
shrouded, damp and secret world. Deep gullies branch off
everywhere. They are fern-filled, with wild fuchsias spilling
out from behind the fern mantle. Ancient mosses girt the old
beech trees like shabby overcoats. Gnarled and twisted lianes

wind up parasitically among the trees. Kie-kie scrambles up the buttressed trunks of pukateas, with climbing rata weaving outside this outside life yet again.

At ground level the kidney ferns lie flat, while the unfolding arms of crown ferns uncoil like the tentacles of a green octopus. There are fungi everywhere, of every hue: bright blue, fiery red, a shocking pink, as if needing this self-advertisement and flamboyance on the forest floor of this dappled and darkly canopied forest world.

There seems to be a bewildering variety of trees and plants wherever one looks. Five-fingered Pseudopanax jostles with fuchsia, wineberry. Nikau palms stand dominant over tangles of supplejack in the deep and secret gullies. From ridge to ridge the patterns change as each species strives for dominance. Upwards the topmost branches of the trees are wreathed in swirls of mist, while the sunlight breaks through in spasms and dapples everything beneath with spangled light. Even the shafts of sunlight seem to be wet.

From high in the trees the raucous notes of the tui sounded brashly, and wherever there was fuchsia or kowhai in flower one could hear the limpid sonorous chimes of the bellbird. Little waxeyes darted everywhere; fantails followed in one's footsteps grateful for the grubs and insects disturbed along the leaf-strewn path.

The track winds upward through the beech forest, then suddenly flattens out through a crunchy woodland glade, then dips into a shallow forested basin before emerging at the lakeside of Waikareiti itself. The lake was first seen by a European in 1871. James Cowan described it as having 'no sign of man; no smoke; no habitation; not even a Maori whare. Little Waikareiti lies as it did in times prehistoric; a spot of great enchantment.' It has little changed to this day.

Here, as one steps out from the bush track to the water's edge, the illusions continue, for this upper lake is itself surrounded by bush-clad hills rising steeply from its shores. The lake is about two miles long, averaging about one mile in width. There are six bush-girt islands set in the lake, on one of which, Rahui, is yet another lake, accessible by tying the boat to the bottom of a rough vertical wooden ladder dangling out of an overhang of rock, then clambering up towards the lake within a lake on the top of the world. This little lake within a lake was known by the Maori as Tamaiti-o-Waikare-iti, 'child of the little rippling water.'

There is a walking track around one-half of Lake Waikareiti, but almost no access for fishing around the steep, bush-clad shoreline other than the little bay at the top of the arrival track, and at Sandy Bay on the far side of the lake, so the only practical way to fish here – and it seems sacrilegious not to – is from a boat.

The Park Headquarters at Aniwaniwa keep a few wooden rowing boats up here. One hires the boat for the day, down at the Headquarters, and is given a key which unlocks a box containing the oars. With such heavy and regular rainfall, the boat will almost always be half-full of water, necessitating the keen exercise of baling out before setting forth upon the lake. But all well worth it. It is well to ponder here at the great feat of getting these heavy wooden boats up there in the first place, but get them there they did.

Waikareiti was stocked with rainbow trout only. No brown trout are present. Suitable spawning streams running into the little lake are limited, yet even without regular stocking the rainbow trout population seems to sustain well. Chief reason for this, of course, is that the water is rarely fished.

It is both prohibited and impossible to get a boat up there (other than the two Park Authority boats for hire), so that at most one would never see more than one other boat out on the water. In all my many visits to Waikaremoana my wife and I always made a sort of pilgrimage up to Waikareiti, and never once saw another boat out. Walkers often climb the track, and hardier trampers frequently round the lake on their way to somewhere else, but few visitors bother to fish Waikareiti as there is better fishing available down below in the big lake –

and with less exertion. Because of this, Lake Waikareiti is very much a wilderness place to fish. But, like all true wildernesses, and just as fly-fishing for trout should always be, it can sometimes be hard fishing.

One might think that, bothered so infrequently by fishermen, the rainbow trout of Waikareiti would be avid takers of the angler's flies. But all fishermen who know such wilderness places know that this is not necessarily the case. It is possible to fish hard all day on Waikareiti without so much as a touch. I know, for I have done so on a few occasions. On such days it only makes sense to think that there are no trout left in the lake, and is somehow defiant of one's sensibilities as an angler to think otherwise.

Then there are times when a mere few pulls on the oars away from the little beach, and a quick cast out into the lake will respond with a good fish on and a lively fight on your hands, for Waikareiti rainbows are lusty creatures. It is one of those waters where the trout seem to come on for no more than a few minutes at a time, then just as suddenly go off, disappearing heaven knows where. This come and go activity seems likely to happen at any time and at any random intervals throughout the day.

Wind and rain are rarely very far away from Waikareiti, but on a bright and sunny day, with a gentle breeze rippling the water, it can seem like paradise. Gliding by the islets is like gliding through a primeval Eden. Fishing is just another way of connecting with it. However slow the fishing seems elsewhere, there is always a good chance of a trout or two in the lovely channels between the islets. The islets themselves have become havens of refuge for at least one survivor from the ravages of the exotic opossums and deer that are ubiquitous everywhere throughout the Park: that is everywhere except on the six islets in Lake Waikareiti. They remain beyond their often destructive reach. Here still grows and prospers the toatoa, considered to be the loveliest of all New Zealand podocarps. This tree has a curious way of growth in that the

140

lower branches sweep down and root where they touch the ground, where they grow to form the stem of a new tree, which repeats the process until a parent tree is often surrounded by a circle of its progeny, for all the world like a natural, living, antipodean stone circle.

It is commonplace that a visitor to such places invariably feels that no one has ever been there before him. A recent comment was: 'Few visitors who have penetrated into its vastness have not returned feeling something of the awe that men always feel in the presence of something primeval. Yet on a sunny day, watching a trout rise in a murmuring river, most would forget this awe, as the mountains have forgotten the warriors – who fought and died under their frowning summits.' Personally, I don't think the mountains have forgotten. But it should be sufficient in such a place just to be there. The trout are by no means monsters, and all seem to weigh in at almost exactly two pounds. Only once do I recall catching and releasing anything smaller, and never anything bigger.

But New Zealand rainbows of two pounds generally belie the quality of the fly-fishing they provide – or of the excellence grilled or barbecued back at the Home Bay camp. For me it is the very sort of fishing I always best remember, long after much supposedly 'better' fishing has been long forgotten.

CROSSING THE RUBICON IN SEARCH OF ALFRED RONALDS

> I find it impossible to pass over the Rubicon without one further mention. If I should fish for a hundred years, I could never again delight in such a priceless piece of novelty as that which befell me, and Fred Stewart, during our next summer break. I have cast a fly upon many waters, but the fishing about which I propose to speak now has had no equal since, nor can it.
>
> **David Scholes,** *The Way of an Angler*

I had just come over from Western Australia where the one and only foray towards a day's fly-fishing turned out to be a total failure. My Australian friends kept telling me that the fishing I had already had in Tasmania and New Zealand was far better than any I might find on the mainland. We had driven for what seemed a long way into Western Australia, only to find what had been described as trout streams, mere trickles. I was with a local fisherman, too. No wonder, it seemed to me in retrospect, that he found most of the solace he had in the sport in fly tying; and most of the exquisite flies he tied would, in all probability, never even get wet.

Back in England a month or two earlier I had been talking to John and Judith Head in that heaven of angling literature they preside over in Salisbury. While I had been a regular client of the Heads for many years, my means are modest, and many fishing books I might drool over are way beyond my means. Unlike some, it is a passion easy to curb, especially in that over the years one may become quite familiar with angling books one will never own.

In this fashion, on that day in Salisbury before the voyage began, I had been admiring particularly fine copies of the splendid two volume set of Alfred Ronalds' *The Fly Fisher's Entomology* in the 1913 limited edition de luxe, with an Introduction by Sir Herbert Maxwell. I was familiar with the book as I had a 10th edition of 1901 in the original format in my own collection, but what was then new and news to me as I looked at the Maxwell edition in John and Judith Head's shop, was something that almost sprang from the last page of the new Introduction.

I had known that the later editions of Ronalds' book in its first format (including my own 10th edition) had been brought out in London by Longmans, the original publisher, at the behest of Alfred Ronalds' brother who had somehow inherited the literary rights to the book even during the author's lifetime. One of the several brief introductions to the various lookalike Longmans editions referred in couched and coded language to the unfortunate fact that Alfred Ronalds had fallen on hard times and had taken himself off in some sort of disgrace. We know that the 3rd edition of 1844 contains an announcement that 'the author prepares for sale the whole series of flies he describes, and also supplies a fly case of new construction.'

Maxwell noted that some time prior to 1844 Ronalds moved from Staffordshire to North Wales where, from an address Dolfanog, Dolgelly, he sold flies to order. We know that his first wife died soon afterwards, and this may be why he emigrated to Ballarat in Australia in 1848, but why the hints of something other in subsequent introductions by his brother in later editions of the book? Maxwell knew that Ronalds started a nurseryman's business in Ballarat. Also that he married again – a Mary Anne Hurlow – by whom he had four children. It seems there were seven children from his first marriage. Of his death in Ballarat we know only that he died of apoplexy.

His brother, still living in Staffordshire, seems to have been suggestive that Alfred had 'disappeared', yet was assiduous in seeing that at least seven more editions were issued, by which time the book had acquired a classic status where it remains to this day as a watershed book in the literature of fly-fishing.

But there, that day in Salisbury in John and Judith Head's bookshop, I turned a page of the Maxwell edition and read the terse, brief statement that Alfred Ronalds had died in Ballarat in Victoria, Australia, in 1860. It seemed about the last place on earth where I might have imagined Alfred Ronalds to be. The mystery remains. What was he doing there? Why had he gone? Had he drifted to Australia in the first place? Had he then been lured to Ballarat in search of gold when the fever and lust for gold was at its height? Had he been forced to leave England? And, if so, why? What had he done? Why did he of all men, with his passion for fly tying and fly-fishing go to this then troutless land on the other side of the world? How had he fared in that gold boom town in inland Victoria? How did he die?

I always intended going to Ballarat one day in search of Alfred Ronalds, to try and solve some of the mystery. But, as it happened, I never got there, and never even got around (as I had long intended) to write to the Registrar of Births and Deaths in that district, and even to fly-fishermen, any of whom might have uncovered some part of the story.

I confess to having an indolent streak right through me, but the real reason I never really persevered in my search for Ronalds was that at about the same time I became interested in another man, Captain George Douglas Hamilton, author of New Zealand's second only fishing book, *Trout Fishing & Sport in Maoriland*, published in Wellington in 1904. Hamilton was an extraordinary man, and seems to have led a most extraordinary life, until he died penniless and broken in Dannevirke in New Zealand in 1911.

The more research I made into Captain Hamilton's life, the stranger and more unlikely it all seemed. Then I realised that everything I knew about him was what he had said about himself. And the more I learned about him, the less I believed almost all of it. Until he died in 1911 in Dannevirke. But even then he escaped me.

When my research began it had all seemed so easy. By then I had found out virtually everything that was officially known about Hamilton, but in going back through all the more obvious records I discovered that all the information on record could be traced back to a few provincial newspaper interviews he gave later on in his life.

In the mid-1850s when New Zealand was a young and sparsely populated colony, contact with the outside world meant that by means of the regular, and ever-increasing, arrivals of sailing ships from Britain and, to a lesser extent, from the not all that much more established new colonies in Australia. The ships might have taken five, six, seven, or even more months to complete the outward voyage. They arrived with new faces, new people, new settlers, cargoes of much-needed goods, seeds, plants, animals – every nail and sheet of iron had to be imported. The arrival of any ship from 'Home' was an event – and full details of every such event were recorded with Victorian thoroughness.

The early newspapers recorded the names of every man, woman and child coming in as passengers, with full details of the ship in which they had travelled, and even of what their intentions were in the young colony. In this fashion the broadsheets were everything from gossip sheets, instant determinants of each new arrival's social station, and advertising medium. Furthermore, the Harbour Boards responsible for running the ports of Dunedin (Port Chalmers), Christchurch (Lyttelton), Wellington and Auckland, as well as the several other relatively important officially designated Ports of Entry, themselves kept detailed records of every ship arriving, listing every person on board, and full details of everyone who disembarked.

But back to George Douglas Hamilton and what he said about himself. Captain Hamilton, as he seemed universally known and seemingly expected to be so addressed, was so large and flamboyant a character, as well as being something of a mystery, that he deserves nothing less than a book to himself. Even then would certainly remain many questionmarks, many doubts, many inconsistencies and unlikelihoods, with perhaps no more than the shadow of the real man flitting through the pages.

George Douglas Hamilton was born in France on 15th July 1835. He was descended from the brother of Lord Hamilton, Regent of Scotland. Educated in France and on the Continent for ten years, he received his further education at Edinburgh University, followed by 'private instruction in permanent fortification and military drawing.' Although receiving a commission in the 11th Hussars in 1851 nothing is known of this episode of his life. It may be noted here that all this happened by the time he was sixteen years of age.

He said he arrived in Wellington on 11th May 1857 and by his own account at once bought himself a horse and rode to Dr Featherston's station at Akitio without a guide and at once took charge of the entire stock there. With the exception of a road of sorts between Wellington and Lower Hutt there was no vestige of road or bridge between Wellington and Napier. In 1858 Hamilton became manager and part stock-owner of St Hill's station at Tukituki, Hawkes Bay. As to his knowledge and past experience of sheep, Hamilton claimed to know more about them than any man then in the Colony. It is about this period that Hamilton's account of his own life once more seems to leave many questions unanswered.

Between 1862 and 1870 Hamilton served as Captain in command of Scouts, Armed Constabulary, Militia and the Maori Contingents in charge of the country between Napier, Taupo, the Upper Waikato, and North and West Urewera;

146

and was present at several engagements and skirmishes during the Maori Wars; being wounded four times and awarded the NZ War Medal.

He 'took up' land in the Mangatoro country near Dannevirke, about 1857 or 1859, then dense bush and reputedly near impenetrable. Later described as an island in a sea of bush, Hamilton leased more than 30,000 acres of land from the Maori. He was the first white settler in the district and appears to have quickly won the respect and esteem of all the local Maori. Hamilton's dream was to create a grand estate, and build a mansion at Mangatoro that would be an antipodean version of the Hamilton ancestral home in Scotland.

He seems to have been an extremely fit and physical sort of man: he talked of challenging all the local Maori to wrestling matches, and quite obviously relished such activities.

He was no doubt a character larger than life, but because all we know about him is what he said about himself in later life it must be accepted that we only have Hamilton's own image of himself. That image was undoubtedly grand and heroic. Most biographies are compiled from an assortment of sources, facts, and the opinions of people who knew the person well, without too much regard – if any – for what the subject of the biography had to say about himself.

In the case of Captain Hamilton the strange fact emerges that we know nothing about him other than what he said about himself. What often appears to be source material turns out to have been copied without comment from a provincial newspaper interview he gave towards the end of his life. In the end it must be accepted that we only have Hamilton's own image of himself.

The few facts that are available seem to be about a different man altogether. Maybe, in disappointed and disillusioned old age, he simply chose to forget some of the more mundane happenings while only remembering the dream: the unfulfilled dream to establish a grand country estate and dynasty in the heartland of the then very new New Zealand.

The Mangatoro Estate was real enough, consisting of 30,750 acres. One gets the impression that to Hamilton himself this was only the beginning, so grand was his view of what he was to hack and hew out of the Seventy Mile Bush. First living in a tent, then a shack, followed by a humble cottage, he then set about building the grand mansion of his dreams. Only the ground floor was ever built – a frontispiece photograph of which is one of the two preliminary pages of his book *Trout Fishing and Sport in Maoriland*. The Mangatoro Stream ran in front of the house. It was stocked with brown trout from Hamilton's private hatchery. In turn most of the streams of the Wairarapa and southern Hawkes Bay were stocked with Mangatoro Hatchery fish. It was thought these were the first brown trout to be introduced into the North Island from ova Hamilton obtained from Otago in 1870.

In the early days Hamilton suffered many reverses of fortune as both the local and more distant Maori tribes objected to the Mangatoro wool clip being transported across their land or down their rivers. He was engaged in constant argument with them over ever-increasing tolls imposed on his wool. The Maori wanted greater payment than the total value of all his wool. At the same time he was engaged in litigation and lawsuits that went on for years, ending sadly in 1910 when the Bank of New Zealand foreclosed on the property, dividing it into twenty farms and grazing runs.

Hamilton emerged a ruined man. He and his wife went to live in an old Maori mill whare at Tiratu, where he died in poverty in 1911.

When I lived in New Zealand I met a lady who was born in one of the larger farms created by the breaking up of the Mangatoro Estate in 1910. She told me she could remember her mother telling her of the pathetic sight of Hamilton, in what must have been the last year of his life, walking the mile or so from Tiratu into Dannevirke, shuffling along, wearing an overlong shabby overcoat, into which capacious inside pock-

148

ets he would put the few things he could afford to buy; a sad and melancholy figure. But even then he was still known as Captain Hamilton.

I searched for the real Captain Hamilton everywhere, but never found him. He escaped from my critical yet sympathetic gaze, just as Alfred Ronalds was to escape from me inland from the wilder shores of Australia. I sought out Hamilton in the records of the Turnbull Library, the National Library, the National Archives, among the masses of newspapers issued between the date of his arrival in New Zealand in 1857 and his death in 1911. I searched through the records of the Wellington Harbour Board – and even other Harbour Boards in case he had landed from a ship in another port, and come to Wellington by some other means.

Not only was he never listed as having been a bona fide passenger arriving in New Zealand by sailing ship, but no ship arrived at Wellington on the date he claimed to have disembarked there, and none within a few weeks of that time. I checked through the passenger lists of every ship arriving in New Zealand in 1857, uncovering hundreds of names of men, women and children, but Hamilton's was not among them.

As to the later assertion that he had served with distinction in the Maori Wars, it is a fact that never was a series of wars recorded in such detail. They were land wars, and colonial policy as well as aspirations needed to be protected. It seems that every name of every private soldier, scout or constable was recorded, along with every excursion undertaken. In going through the histories and records of the fighting in all the same areas Hamilton claimed he commanded I found literally hundreds of names – but never once the name Hamilton, let alone George Douglas Hamilton. What was the truth?

The litigation and lawsuits against him by the Bank of New Zealand were all too true, as was the Bank's foreclosure on the Mangatoro Estate. But virtually nothing else. I certainly could not track down his birth certificate, although I did find

149

a record of his wife's – but, of his wife, Hamilton himself never even mentioned her existence. Instead, he talked of the faithful manservant who had stood by him through the wars and all the years of hardship in building the estate and the houses. Hamilton described how he decided to keep the rude shack in which he had lived (after the first tent), as well as the humble wooden cottage that followed, as a memorial of sorts and a reminder to those who came after him of what it had been like for the founder of it all. But this faithful old manservant had destroyed both the shack and the cottage because he could not bear to think that people coming after them would see the rude and humble places where Captain George Douglas Hamilton first lived. At least that is the story Hamilton himself told in later years.

The irony of it all is that not one single trace of the grand house remains standing. I went there to look for at least something. All I found that seemed to hint of once grander notions of the landscape were two lines of trees, with enough of them left standing and living to see they had once marked out the avenue of the long curving sweep of the drive up to the house that had simply vanished from the face of the earth – as if it had never been – as if even the substance of the dream had crumbled in its own ashes. But there are still brown trout in the stream below the house site.

All I found was Captain Hamilton's death certificate.

From there I went to find him in the parish churchyard, but he eluded me even there. There is but a single cemetery in the town, so if Hamilton had been buried in Dannevirke, I would be able to find his grave. I reasoned that, even if I couldn't find the real man as he was in life, I would find him in his death. But once again I was wrong. He eluded me even then.

I found his son's grave there, but the headstone told me nothing. There was no way of linking the son to the father. For one thing, during his lifetime Hamilton never even mentioned that he had a son – or a wife, for that matter.

I walked the long straight rows of graves, noting each and

every headstone. After exhausting all that part of the cemetery obviously used around the time of his death, but finding
no trace of him, I set about the task quite systematically.
Starting at the very first grave in the very first row I followed
a close grid, until I came to the very last grave. Was he not
buried there? And, if not, where else might he have been
buried? In a pauper's grave? Were there such things as pauper's graves in New Zealand in 1911?

Looking for Captain Hamilton among those neat rows of
hundreds of gravestones was an odd experience, to say the
least. The symmetry of pattern was quite extraordinary. Each
plot was the same size. The paths between the lines of plots
were absolutely straight and absolutely identical. Even the
headstones seemed to be of remarkable similarity, in a place
where more often, elsewhere, no two adjoining memorials are
the same.

As I walked the long straight lines, ever watchful for my
man, I could see behind to the next row of graves, and beyond
them, to the next, and so on. A visual pattern akin to optical
illusion registered in my brain, almost hallucinating in the endless repetition of images. Suddenly, all the gravestones
seemed to start moving, waving, weaving, leaning, rippling,
swaying, as if they were afloat upon the seas of eternity, as if
their occupants were stirring in the earth beneath. I know that
sounds far-fetched, but swear it to be absolutely true. Had I
merely become giddy, mesmerised, by the concentration and
high hopes of what turned out to be a fruitless search?

I shall never know, but there in the Dannevirke cemetery I
gave up my search for Captain Hamilton and have never since
resumed it. Did it all happen the way he said it did? Was he
in any real way the man he said he was? All I know with cer-
tainty is that he wrote New Zealand's second angling book.
Nowadays it is a rare book, although copies of it do turn up
from time to time with surprising regularity. My own copy is
signed by Hamilton himself. The inscription is in a bold flowing hand and reads: "Best regards to my old friend Mack

Captain Hamilton".

Loosely inserted is a small and faded sepia photograph – a mere two inches by one inch – of a full rigged sailing ship under way, and I sometimes wonder as to its possible significance, or even insignificance, as so often happened in my search for Captain Hamilton.

❉ ❉ ❉ ❉ ❉

And, in much the same way, all my searches for Alfred Ronalds in Australia led me up blind paths. Had I not become disillusioned in my search for Captain Hamilton in Scotland and New Zealand I might have persevered and gone to Ballarat. Somehow, it always seemed, I was chasing willo'the wisps, shadows, not real men.

Whatever the truth may have been, as I seemed to get closer to it, the details blurred. The more I found out that in both cases there appeared to be so many skeletons hidden away in secret cupboards I was seeking to unlock, the more it seemed unseemly to continue prying into these men's lives. This is probably why I stopped searching for them. To leave their ghosts in peace.

I have already written how that happened with me for Captain Hamilton. This is how it happened in the case of Alfred Ronalds.

❉ ❉ ❉ ❉ ❉

My attempts to pin-point Ronalds to Ballarat had always been of no avail. When thousands of men, women, and children, poured into Victoria through ships arriving in Melbourne and Geelong, on their way to seeking fortunes of gold at Ballarat, there were none of the social niceties of listing every incoming passenger by name in the newspapers and Harbour Board records. Things were done rougher in Australia in those days. Many were escaping from pasts they would prefer to forget. It was easy enough for anyone to change his or her name to anything they chose. It was easy enough for anyone to change their past and lineage, and to begin to live out any dream they wanted.

Was Hamilton living out such a dream? Was Ronalds merely retreating from whatever bad dream England had left him with? I did not get to Ballarat, but someone I knew in Melbourne told me that he remembered reading – although he could not remember where – that Alfred Ronalds had fished the Rubicon River for trout. Now the Rubicon is a tributary of the Goulburn River, itself a tributary in turn of the Murray River. Melbourne lies at the apex of a triangle with the Rubicon in one corner and the town of Ballarat at the other, about a hundred miles to the west. Brown trout were first introduced into Victoria in 1864 in the famous Norfolk ship-ment donated by Francis Francis and Frank Buckland. By 1877 trout fry had been planted in many river systems throughout Victoria, right to the Snowy Mountains. Much of it was centered upon the thriving Ballarat Fish Acclimatisation Society where liberations of young trout began as early as 1871.

We know that before the first edition of Alfred Ronalds' *The Fly-Fisher's Entomology*, in 1836 he was noted for his knowledge of 'entomological and piscatorial science,' and that on the River Blythe – 'A sweet trout-stream in Staffordshire' – Ronalds had built his 'Observatory' for the closer study of trout. Whatever actually took him to Ballarat, it seems incon-ceivable that if he was there during the first heady days of acclimatisation, and the beginnings of trout fishing there, he was not somehow drawn into the grand experiment. He was certainly more expert in the ways of trout than anyone then in Ballarat. Yet, in all the fairly copious and detailed literature of those events, Ronalds' name is unmentioned – as indeed, sim-ilarly, that he had ever been there.

I could have kicked my informant in Melbourne for the fact that although he was certain he had read somewhere that

Alfred Ronalds had fished the Rubicon River, he could not remember the source of this knowledge. As if to placate my exasperation he telephoned me a few days later, to ask if I would care to join him on a fishing trip to the Rubicon next day. Naturally, I jumped at the chance.

The day we went there was Melbourne Cup Day, so we thought that all Australia, let alone Victoria, would be at the races, or at least glued to their television sets, leaving us the freedom of the river. It turned out to be a delightful little stream, low in the early summer drought, but gin clear.

We fished dry flies, stalking the water as we edged upstream, but never once actually spotted a trout. In a couple of hours fishing, when fishing the water in likely looking lies, I caught and released one small brown trout and lost another of better size under a partly submerged log on the opposite side. Lloyd, my companion, did approximately likewise, but the fish he released was upwards of a pound, and the fish he lost looked to be all of three, but may have been less. We fished from soon after nine o'clock that morning until six in the evening, apart from stopping for a splendid family barbecue. I should have enjoyed the fishing day more than I did. The trouble was I was really looking for Alfred Ronalds, not trout. Did I somehow expect that on one particular cast I would catch something of the man, rather than a trout?

Suffice it to say that if I was really searching for Ronalds I never found him – not there in Australia or anywhere else for that matter in the days that followed.

I crossed and re-crossed the Rubicon many times in search of him. Maybe, after all, that was enough.

A TALE OF THREE RIVERS

The voices of the subterranean river in the shadows were different from the voices of the sunlit
river ahead. In the shadows against the cliff the
river was deep and engaged in profundities, circling
back on itself now and then to say things over to be
sure it had understood itself. But the river ahead
came out into the sunny world like a chatterbox,
doing its best to be friendly. It bowed to one shore
and then to the other so nothing would feel neglect-
ed. By now I could see inside the sunshine and had
located my father. He was sitting high on the bank . .
. He was reading, although evidently only by sentences because he often looked away from the book.
He did not close the book until some time after he
saw me. I scrambled up the bank and asked him,
'How many did you get?' He said, 'I got all I want.'
I said, 'But how many did you get?'. He said, 'I got
four or five.' I asked, 'Are they any good?' He said,
'They are beautiful.' . 'What have you been reading?'
I asked. 'A book,' he said. It was on the ground on
the otherside of him. So I would not have to bother to look over his knees to see it, he said, 'A good
book.' Then he told me, 'In the part I was reading it
says the word was in the beginning, and that's right.
I used to think water was first, but if you listen

carefully you will hear that the words are under-
neath the water.'
        Norman Maclean, *A River Runs Through It*

In those days we went in privately. That is to say we went in through private land, through the vast lands of one of the biggest stations in the North Island of New Zealand. A pri- vate road went in, mile after mile through tussocky high coun- try: sheep country, still in the days when the sheep was central to the New Zealand economy, although even then the writing was on the wall; Britain was now in the Common Market and New Zealand would never be the same again.

Bill and Nick knew the owner of this huge pastoral station. To me, at first, after I'd met them, he and his family seemed unlikely people to be running such a near wilderness place, but they fitted it perfectly inspite of the seeming unlikelihood of it all; the homestead itself an island of comfort and charm deep in the heart of the land. The owner was a most pleasant and cultured man, descended from Stanley Baldwin – Earl Baldwin of Bewdley – Prime Minister of Great Britain on the one hand, and from Rudyard Kipling on the other. And here he was with an even more charming Canadian wife in the very heart of the North Island of New Zealand owning and run- ning a sheep station bigger than some English counties, assist- ed by a couple of handsome red-headed sons who seemed cast in the mould of modern, high- tech, airplane-and helicopter- flying Huckleberry Finns.

For me the journey in was like a trip to paradise. We only called in at the house to make our number and let them know when we expected to come out again, then continued on as far as the road – now diminished to a rough track – went into the hills, until we got as far as we could go before walking in to where we planned to make camp. It was at the junction of three rivers: two, really, because the Oamaru River leads out of the western valley and is joined by the Kaipo River, a rugged mountain trout stream if there ever was one, bordering the station boundary and the Kaimanawa State Forest Park to the west and the Kaweka State Forest Park to the south across this interlinking network of fast mountain rivers.

A mile downstream the newly augmented river is joined by another stream, the Taharua River, tumbling in to add to its increasing flow yet again. Here the single, enlarged and enhanced river takes on another, different name, the Mohaka, a big river, a giant among rivers that will, along its long coursing through some of the most rugged country in the North Island, be itself increased by other tributary rivers as famed as the Waipunga, Ripia, and Te Hoe before entering the Pacific Ocean in the great sweep of Hawkes Bay to the east.

Leaving the cars on a high bluff overlooking the newly born Mohaka River we tramped in with backpacks down to the narrow strip of valley flat below where the Oamaru, Kaipo and Mohaka Rivers become one. There we set up our tents and made camp on a little tussocky rise, not more than fifty yards from the river. Even as we put up the tents and stored our food and gear we could hear the inviting gurglings and splutterings of the newborn Mohaka and see the golden flashes of sparkling sunlight reflected back from its running waters.

With such invitingness at hand and out there together in that vast loneliness it was not long before we left the camp chores undone and set off upstream with our fly rods.

We waded across the very topmost run of the Mohaka River itself, before it becomes the Oamaru immediately above the fast undercliff reach we intended to fish. There – almost more in the manner of performing a ritual first fishing – we each in turn had a few casts upstream into the sunlit waters. Nick first. We watched as a trout streaked out from under the topmost white water as his nymph tumbled down the stream, but the fish turned away from it, heading back up into the fastneess of the head of the pool. After a few such ritual casts it was my turn to have some sacramental casts of my own, but only once did I actually see a rainbow come out after the sink-

157

ing nymph before changing its mind. Next, came Richard, Nick's son, and with his second cast was fast into a leaping rainbow that cavorted around the pool on its tail before bearing down to the bottom and running everywhere but right out of its home pool. He soon had it in the net: a nice rainbow of about three pounds, skilfully unhooked by means of Nick's medical forceps and released with no harm done to it. Bill, who would have rather moved on, cast a dry coch-y-bondhu up into the white water but the trout that rose to it was only half-interested, so he reeled up and we moved upstream for the start of more serious fishing.

Nick and Richard took the Oamaru, while Bill and I went upstream into the more heavily wooded Kaipo. And there I found a trout stream of superlative delight: everything a trout stream should be: not too big, not too small: not too brawling, not too meadow-like; not too fast, not too slow. Just pure delight as we made our way up through gradually ascending runs and riffles and pools, each and every one a delight to fish as the stream turned and bent and made its way through long glades of dappled sunlight under the canopy of native bush and fern that sometimes made a tunnel of the stream.

But, there were open stretches, too: bouldery runs and pocket water with no cover, opening up to long vistas of enchantment looking up the valley going up into the hills where the river was born beyond the Cascade Stream on the Kaipo Saddle in the Kaimanawas. Sheer delight. The realisation of dreams.

When Stephen Hawking was pondering how to put into layman's words the worlds and universes inside his head of quantum physics and the ultimate cosmology he asked the question, why if we can remember the past can't we remember the future? It seemed essential to his view of *A Brief History of Time*.

Readers of a few of these tales of fishing might be forgiven for questioning why – at least in some of them – it has been suggested that, somehow, the present clock and calendar time of everyday existence seemed fused with past experience, with time already passed, yet almost as if it was all part of something yet to happen. It was further suggested that in certain somehow favoured places the very act of fishing was sometimes a route into such experience, and that perhaps a fly rod was the magic wand that somehow led the fisherman towards that strange other, floating, world.

Uncommonly difficult though it may be to express – even to fellow anglers – and conscious, too, that to some it must sound like bunkum – the Kaipo River was such a place. Nothing I experienced there seemed to be happening now. Most things appeared to have happened before, in much the same way one might suddenly recall the substance of an earlier dream. Yet, and parallel with that strange feeling of it being time remembered, there was the opposite feeling that one was experiencing some future tomorrow.

Whether it was more to do with temporary hallucination brought on by doing something so blissful in the state of mind it induced, I shall never know. All that I do know, and can say with complete honesty, is that it was just like that that day on the Kaipo. It was another of those very special days.

It may be even more connected with Thoreau's view that many men go fishing all of their lives without knowing it is not the fish they are after.

After fishing up through several enchanted pools together on that first day, Bill and I split up. He went on ahead much further upstream, bypassing the river altogether, in having found a track that went straight on by several great twists and bends in the stream that would lead him back to the higher reaches, leaving me to fish up alone through a multitude of undisturbed, untroubled and unfished pools. Each succeeding pool and run seemed to lead me to even more enchanting bliss.

A quality of catch-and-release uncommented upon, it seems, in other writing of which I am aware, is the liberating freedom it brings from that pressing sense of urgency and indecent haste that comes with most fishing nowadays. I have said before that it is one thing to catch-and-release a good trout in front of either another confirmed catch-and-release fisherman – or even in full view of an admiring and almost nonbelieving throng of non-angler tourists, as once I observed a well-known angler do, and quite another thing altogether to catch-and-release such a trout when one is quite alone on a remote high country stream, with no one to witness this rite of compassion and conservation.

But what I mean now by that other quality it brings, is somewhat different. If one is quite alone fishing up through paradisal pools and runs, intent on fishing as well and as cunningly as possible, yet knowing in advance that one will carefully release unharmed each and every trout one catches, irrespective of size, and just as irrespective of one's possible hunger to eat such a trout or – should it be a very special one – to keep it as a prize or trophy. After all many wise anglers have observed that the fish he catches are the fisherman's reward; the currency in which he is paid.

But – if a fly-fisherman has predetermined that, because he is fishing where he is, he will always and automatically return each and every fish he catches back to the water unharmed – he will fish as if a yoke has been removed from his shoulders. He may still be a deceitful cunning bastard, setting out to deceive the trout with his hooked confection of fur and feather, and there may even be some retrospective satisfaction in doing so. But what will have disappeared is all the haste and anxiety that normally burdens so many fishermen; and an indecent haste at that, to catch a limit bag as soon as possible; and an ugly anxiety, moreover, because lack of success is associated with abject failure and self-depreciation. Worse still, that it has been a waste of time.

For such an angler freed from these burdens the act of going fishing takes on a new and different light. Far from the nagging indecent haste to pull some trout out as fast as possible, the fisherman will do what he ought have done all along. Approached the new pool quietly, slowly, cautiously. Then, having hidden himself away in some vantage point, sat there quietly for ten minutes or so, watching and getting acquainted with the pool in front of him. He will certainly see trout that otherwise, had he strode straight into its tail and begun casting, would have been put down. And by spooking just one fish in that pool, the balanced tenure of that strictly territorial small environment and circumscribed ecosystem will be upset, with disturbing, unsettling waves of action and reaction caused by the over-hasty fisherman-intruder affecting all the creatures living there.

How much better to sit, unseen, unheard, unsuspected, and wait. And the chances are that within ten minutes the various territorial boundaries of most of the inhabitants of the pool will have been mapped out, and the quiet observer of the scene know a great deal more about the ways and means of those inhabitants than he would have done had he fished straight up through it immediately on arrival.

Similarly, too, from his concealed vantage point, the watcher of the pool will have calculated from where best to cast in order to get nymph or dry fly into a position most likely to interest a feeding trout, and how deep he needs to get it, in the case of a sunk nymph, or along which food line he needs to float his artificial if it is to be a dry fly or a nymph hanging in the surface film. There will be times during such watching and waiting when the actual insect on which the trout are feeding can be identified and matched.

If more than one trout is sighted he will know which one to go for first. He may even estimate about how many chances he might have before reeling up and passing on, and he may have gleaned some awareness of where a hidden trout or two might be lying in deeper, darker water, or tucked up in the shadow of an undercut bank. By the seemingly bothered unsettled patrolling of a particular fish, or by the steady, regular, untroubled, unbothered way a trout holds underwater station, feeding constantly on a variety of passing morsels rather than only occasionally and selectively, the observant angler will know whether to move on after a few casts, or persistently and pesteringly put a fly over a particular trout's nose until it takes it. All these are things unknown and unobserved by the fisherman in a hurry to begin casting.

Watched in such unhurried ways pools that seem empty of trout or any other life, for that matter, at first glance, come alive. Birds, otherwise missed, are seen on and about the water: iridescent flash of kingfisher, the bouncing antics of the tui, the sonorous bellbird, cheeky fantail, darting silvereye, can well atone for the occasional fishless pool and make the wait worthwhile. In any case, the chances are that some pools will be fishless – about which cause and reason our observant angler might well ponder on – but because that burden and urgency to catch and kill trout has been removed, they will no longer seem like abject disappointments and wasters of time.

There can be little doubt that the best way to be fly-fishing is without unseemly urgency or haste or greed or even hope of too much reward. And, in such cases, the chances are the fisherman will fish the better for it, paradoxically catching more fish, finding satisfactions and delights previously undreamed of, as well as modest skills he thought had been denied him. In some such fashion I fished up through the Kaipo Stream that day. There were no disappointments, no frustrations, simply a marvellous sense of well-being. It seemed as if life itself had been slowed down, as if all of nature was in slow motion, not wanting the passing hours to signal the end of the day, prolonging it into an everlasting present.

In such blissful mood I fished on through the afternoon, in some ways almost reluctant to leave off in one pool and move on to the next. In all I suppose I connected with six or eight trout: a couple but briefly; a few for a little longer; and three landed and returned: all rainbows and all about three pounds. I got them all from pools of dappled sunlight, or at least part-dappled sunlight where there was a canopy of mountain beech and great tree ferns skirting the deep side of the pools, casting shadows while the sunlight was uninterrupted on the other side where shallows of pebbly gravels led out to bars of sand. And the fish all took along that shimmering line between the dappled shadows and the plain full sunlight.

But my fishing was totally unhurried and unpressed, as if it was an episode that had no beginning and would have no end; not so much in a timeless sort of way, but rather as if time itself was suspended.

Fishing in one such shadowy dappled paradise several hours on into the late afternoon, when the air was cooling fast and the shadows lengthening, Bill suddenly materialised out of the bush, his happy grin speaking volumes that he, too, had had all he sought further upstream. I use the word materialise for the manner in which he suddenly appeared through the forest clearing, as if out of nowhere, but with full intention. Some people crash and burst their way through such country. One hears notice of their coming from half a mile off, as if they are alien to the place. Bill, on the other hand, is the best such man I know for the uncanny ability he has to slide through such places, hardly rustling a leaf.

There is that sage admonition that people who go in to wilderness places should leave nothing behind but their footprints. Bill seems to better that, and wherever possible never even leaves behind his footprints to show where he has gone. He made me mindful of the Taoist couplet of Chuang Tzu:

> Entering the forest without moving the grass;
> Entering the water without raising a ripple.

Bill, too, had found everything he sought along the river. In a wordless sort of way we each knew the other was well content, and with the onset of tiredness after such a day, ready to make our way back to our camp. As we waded across the young Mohaka River below we chanced upon two trampers coming the other way: a young man and a young woman. After exchanging some words with them we went on our separate ways. In a reflective sort of way Bill said that he had much admired the girl's shapely legs encased in the stout tramping boots and woollen socks. She carried a pack as big and heavy as any Sherpa.

Our camp was on the other side of the river, which we now re-crossed over the thigh-deep shallows. Nick and Richard were already back. They, too, had had a good day up the Oamaru. They had a fire going, tea brewing, and the beginnings of our evening meal already under way. The whisky out of plastic mugs with a little branch water straight out from the Mohaka, Kaipo, Oamaru confluence tasted good. Normally, neither Nick nor Bill cared to drink streamwater cupped with the hands straight out of the river, as I did, although it always seemed to me that the water in such places was purer than from any urban tap. Still, they were right and wiser about it, for in their reasoning a deer or wild pig or strayed sheep gone wild might have fallen to its death in the river somewhere upstream, making it unsafe to drink. In such remote back-country, with no easy way out except on one's feet, was no place to be stricken with any illness. The whisky and branch water still tasted good. As, too, did our meal an hour later.

By the time the last light was fading from the sky, and a rolling bank of low cloud came rolling in from the west, bringing a short sharp series of rain showers, we had doused our fire, climbed into our sleeping bags in the snug tents and given thanks for such a day, and just to be there in such a perfect place.

We were surrounded by night-sounds: some of which we recognised and understood, while others were alien to us. We heard the incessant plaintive call of the morepork, the native owl, with its repeated cry of 'morepork', 'morepork', 'morepork'. We heard the roar of a stag that came from the flat-browed hill across the river, repeated again from behind us on the other side from the slope above the Poronui Hut. The small dark mayflies we had observed before dark, celebrating their nuptial dance in a great swarm around an incongruous looking, scraggy and isolated manuka bush close by our tents, continued. While our tent lantern was still lit we could hear the light thrumming of the teeming mayflies against the taut fabric of the tent fly sheet. Bill thought he heard the unmistakable sound of wild pigs nosying around our campsite. But even marauding Captain Cookers would not have kept me awake that night and I slept the sleep of a well contented man.

Next morning there was just a hint of frost as we busied ourselves preparing breakfast and readying ourselves for the day. Soon afterwards we were off again, fly rods in hand and day backpacks containing food and drink. This time Bill and I took the upstream waters of the Oamaru River, while Nick and Richard went up the Kaipo.

The Oamaru was quite a different river. Several washed-down trees from previous storms lay across the river – creating lies and pools within pools for trout – into which a well-pitched nymph might gain a positive response and almost certain hooking, although the submerged debris and underwater branches made it just as easy for the trout to make its assured getaway.

It was a good river and a good fishing day, although by comparison with the Kaipo I found little magic in it. I seem to remember from later conversations that the other three preferred the Oamaru as a trout stream. And they were all better fishermen than I. But for me it lacked that certain magic. However good the fishing might have or have not been, for me at least I got no response from it of being a special place that awoke in me any of that rare reaction to the spirit of the place. Which is a pity and regretful to me, because in so doing I undoubtedly do the Oamaru Stream a grave injustice it does not deserve.

I wonder whether, had I fished the Oamaru first, then the Kaipo next day, my feelings might have been otherwise. But this I shall never know, and shouldn't read too much into it. It was all a matter of unfair comparisons. Maybe I expected the Oamaru would duplicate, replicate the Kaipo, but with anything so rare as to whatever it was, the feeling I got, fishing through the Kaipo pools, it would be foolhardy to expect the same sense and awareness of place, the same magic, on two successive days in two successive adjacent rivers.

The day following we all went downstream along the Mohaka, fishing up through runs and pools as they took our fancy. It was exciting fishing at the Taharua confluence, where the tributary stream cascades down across a great bouldery spillway of white water into the burgeoning Mohaka. On the true right hand bank a narrow ledge of great boulders gives way to a sheer vertical cliff face of hard basaltic rock. Incredibly, in fissures in the towering rockface grow out large overhanging flax bushes in what appears to be a tenuous foothold and a fragile, unlikely place for great flax to prosper. Yet it does.

On the opposite bank, where the Taharua roars in over its uplifted natural spillway, on either side of which great fronds of toitoi arch into the air, shimmering in the breeze, sparkling like gold in the bright sunlight. A shelving bank behind the toitoi is dense with manuka, stretching up the lower slopes of the mountainside until, with altitude, it yields to gorse and scatterings of stunted beech trunks like the grey ghosts of old forgotten totem poles.

I was able to fish downstream from behind the upper stands of toitoi, changing over to a sinking line and allowing the lure to tumble downstream in the young Mohaka, then out into the fast white water of the Taharua at its very end, where it ceases to have a separate existence and its own name. Once I had a rainbow take my proferred Red Setter and charge off with it downstream, into the fast water. That rainbow trout exploded out into the air just once in an arching leap, then kept on going until I could do nothing more than point my rod tip at the rapidly departing fish and hold on until the leader parted and the brief but exciting episode was ended.

For anyone excited by white-foaming, tumbling water, and the prospective delights of somehow casting a fly along the edges of it, this place is at once a delight and a terrible frustration. Delight because the prospects seem endless, but frustration because of the sheer impossibility of getting a fly into any of those inviting places. Hereabouts we have arrived at a place beyond the physical boundaries and possible limits of fly-fishing. The fisherman, having got to this extremity of place and purpose, as I was, can do no more than come away suitably humbled, suitably belittled, by the awesomeness of the place, but thankful that he has been there.

And so we fished on in other places from that camp until it was time to pack up, take down the tents, and climb the steep hill again to the cars parked beyond the very end of this track to nowhere. Yet, to me, it was somewhere very special.

At the time I was gravely disappointed that I did not fish the Kaipo Stream once more before we tramped out. As it happened, for a variety of reasons all beyond my control, I never fished there again.

But writing this now, in having said what I've said, written what I've written, and sung a song in its praise, I am glad. That is just how it should be. In any case magic like that, and perfection of place, together with the timing of it and the nature of the day in question, are tenuous, rarely achievable experiences. Better, I'd say, to remember just how it was, just once. On one particular day.

SHADES OF
THE ROGUE RIVER

One cannot ever forget the presence of the Tongariro. At first it kept me awake at night, just as the rumbling of the volcano Ngauruhoe did last year, when we camped on Lake Taupo. My first fishing was at sunrise next morning after our arrival. There had been frost on the grass and the tang of autumn in the air. Rosy clouds overhung the mountain. The river was shimmering. And as I waded in, shrinking, for I remembered that water, I had the shock of ice into my very marrow. But I waded and cast. Had there been any one to see me surely he would have guessed that I had been sea fishing for long. It was hard for me to get any distance, and as always, I never could seem to be ready for a rise. Suddenly my rod ducked, the line zipped out of my left hand – whizz – splash! and a big red rainbow, jaws open like a wolf, leaped high and threw the hook, and soused back. I gasped, thrilled. "How do. Much obliged to meet you. Why such a hurry?" I exclaimed. All the same, I very soberly worked out in my mind a calculation as to the size of that trout. He could easily have swallowed some of the steelhead in the Rogue River, Oregon.

Zane Grey, *Tales from a Fisherman's Log*
(1978) from edited diaries chronicling his 1927
'expedition' to New Zealand.

The coast of the Pacific Northwest is inextricably bound up
in my conversion to fly-fishing. It was in a downtown
sporting goods store in Seattle I bought my first fly rod: an
early Eagle claw hollow fibreglass eight-footer that served me
well and wove its spell about me, as compelling now as then.
Somewhere along the way that particular fly rod disappeared,
but the fly reel I bought that day in Seattle – a Pflueger
Medalist – is with me still. It is as good as ever, although I
must confess that I have not used it for more than twenty
years, for reasons most fly-fishermen will recognize and even
own up to. I suppose that in some harmless sort of way it is to
do with certain snobberies in the matter of fishing tackle. The
demise of use, but not the disappearance, of that perfectly
good Eagle Claw fly rod came about in this manner.

There cannot be an angler who does not hanker for yet one
more rod; convinced that only then will he be minimally but
adequately equipped for his essential, immediate needs. The
circumstances of my work in those days meant that virtually
all my fly-fishing was done in Tasmania, New Zealand, and
frequent but briefer occasions somewhere along the Pacific
Northwest, even as far as Alaska. I had few, indeed, opportunities in those days to fish in Britain: the odd day at Darwell
or Powdermill in Sussex, or even less frequent days and nights
after sea trout. But, for every day I had the chance to fish in
my home country, I had ten or more to fish in more exotic
places. Not unnaturally, my mind's eye as far as fly-fishing
was concerned, was more influenced – both in fact, and imagination and anticipation – by the Tongariro River, the
Mohaka, Campbell River, Deschutes, Stillaguamish, Skagit,
Coquitlam, Kispiox, the Russian, Eel, the Umpqua, and the
Rogue – especially, at that time, the Rogue.

In those early days I was still intoxicated by the Zane Grey myth. But that was before I had time and inclination as well as opportunity to research the man, starting with his New Zealand Eldorado fishing 'expeditions', that proved to have been not exactly what he made them seem. I had seen the Tongariro once before that but never fished it. That was to come, next week. But even then I longed to fish the Rogue.

Although I know in retrospect that my old Eagle Claw fly rod was more than adequate to fish anywhere I was likely to go, I had increasing doubts at the time that it was perhaps no match at all for the work I eagerly anticipated providing it with: I was hankering and lusting after a more powerful and more appropriate weapon. For in those days I was still in that stage where I regarded a fly rod as a 'weapon'.

At that time the Hardy catalogues I regarded as essential reading had neither become glossy again after the gloomy dull days that followed the end of the war, nor really contained anything new; and what there was invariably went for export only. It was in this fashion that I had long been aware of – and coveted – a Hardy split cane "Rogue River" fly rod. But I had never seen or handled one, except vicariously in the pages of Hardy's catalogue.

Then one day I found myself in Christchurch in New Zealand, in Tisdall's sporting goods store, and in their small rack of fly rods stood an assembled "Rogue River". To me it shone like Excalibur's sword. It was beautiful, and I fell in love with it at once. The salesman, a wiser fly-fisherman than I, was prudently suggesting that, for the sort of fishing I had described to him, I might be better advised to buy the Hardy "LRH Dry Fly" split cane rod that stood next to the "Rogue River" in the rod rack. The prices were about the same. But I was a gonner even then, for I was entranced by the very aura of the "Rogue River" long before I ever saw the actual river of that name. Zane Grey had done his work on me, and I was sold on the "Rogue River". I had to have it. And did.

As it happened the "Rogue River" fly rod served me well,

although I might have made a wiser choice, and one not entirely dictated by an understandable, but not very logical attachment to those magic names, Rogue River and Zane Grey. It led me to many memorable places. With it I caught my first Tongariro trout. Over the next few years it brought many good trout and sea trout to my net, and not a few salmon, from a host of rivers and lakes throughout New Zealand, Tasmania, the mainland of Australia, South Africa, Britain, Canada, the United States – even, towards the end of its working life, from the famed and fabled Rogue River itself.

It was a heavy rod for me to wield all day long, and undoubtedly took much abuse over the next few years. Then I bought a good fibreglass Hardy Smuggler and a couple of different weight Fenwick backpack fly rods, and was at once liberated from the tyranny of weight. Soon after that I bought the first of several early carbon fibre rods: some good; some not so good. The conversion was almost complete. I put away the "Rogue River" more than twenty years ago, promising myself – and the rod – that it would be given an occasional outing and some work to do. But, since that day, I have never taken that rod out of its cloth bag – not even to look at it with a certain nostalgia – not even to set it up and flex its power; not even to show it the light of day, anywhere, let alone on the Rogue River.

Most of us have certain well meaning intentions lurking around in the backs of our minds. One of mine is that I must take out my old "Rogue River" fly rod from its bag, and set it up and handle it again, if only for the memories it will evoke. But I never seem to get around to doing so. In recent years I have dispensed with a certain amount of unwanted tackle – surprisingly, to me, a magpie of fishing gear, without much emotional heartache – yet know that I could never sell, and probably never bring myself to give away, my old "Rogue River" fly rod. It is now a talisman of sorts; both too much a part of things that were important to me, as well as a reminder of uninformed, partly snobbish, partly infantile innocence of earlier fishing days. Like Walton I still incline to the view that angling is a pastime of innocence.

❖ ❖ ❖ ❖ ❖

The road that more or less follows the Oregon coastline rolls on by great mountain spurs and rugged headlands, with long, curving sandy beaches interspersing the wilder bluffs. Great waves surf in from far across the wide Pacific, thundering and breaking over the rocks and seaward headlands. The golden beaches are piled with the driftwood, flotsam and debris of unending successions of ocean storms.   There is a misty, hazy grandeur in the landscape, making this coast as immediately recognisable as any I know.

For many years before I saw it from the coastal road itself, I had been familiar with this landscape as observed from the sea, so often wreathed in mist, often dense fog, and – despite shipboard radar – always welcome to the navigator the splendid succession of famous lighthouses between Cape Flattery and San Francisco. They were melodic names to me as a navigator, even before I read the same names in Zane Grey and other writers' books.   La Push, Tillamook, Cascade Head, Coos Bay, Yaquina Head, Cape Blanco, Gold Beach, then southwards still, along the coast of northern California, past Point St George, Klamath, Trinidad Head, Eureka, Cape Mendicino, to Rockport, Caspar and Elk, Point Arena, and on to San Francisco Bay. The coastal range is relatively low; few peaks higher than about 4000 feet. The range is cut by several rivers flowing through narrow passes and steep valleys to the sea. The rivers are often named after the Indian sub-tribes who once lived along their banks: Nehalem, Nestucca, Siletz, Yaquina, Alsea, Siuslaw, Umpqua, Coos, Coquille, and Rogue; then, once into California, the Klamath, Eel, the Russian.

I had always hoped and planned to get into this region from the north, taking advantage of frequent visits to Seattle and Tacoma, but it never came about that way. Instead, it was to

172

be from San Francisco, from the south. I have indeed been most fortunate in often having good and kind friends among the shore establishments of the shipping agencies looking after the interests of the ships I served in. And in this manner I had several times been out on long holiday weekends, and other occasional periods of waiting, from San Francisco southwards through Monterey and Carmel, as far along the Mission coast as San Luis Obispo; inland through Sacramento to Lake Tahoe, and Lahontan in Nevada; and through the Yosemite and on to Death Valley.

But these particular hosts were not anglers, and we mostly stuck to the tourist trail, for they, too, an expatriate English family, were relatively new to life in San Francisco. On the very last of that particular period of trans-Pacific voyages from New Zealand, the ship was to lie idle in San Francisco throughout a long holiday weekend. Chris and his wife said to me, "Where would you like to go? Name the place!" It didn't take long for me to reply, "Would the Rogue River be too far? I've always wanted to go there, and hopefully fish the river, if only in a token sort of way."

First thing next morning we were on our way out of San Francisco, heading north to join Highway 5 towards Medford. San Francisco Bay had been shrouded in thick fog, but once past Napa, travelling the inland Highway, the day began to shine. We seemed to fly through the Sacramento Valley, on past the Shasta Dam, and soon across the state border into Oregon, and on to Medford.

As so often happens in life, I only wish now that my research into Zane Grey as an angler had begun by then. As it was, at that time I still regarded him as having been the greatest fly-fisherman of all time; which, in fact, he wasn't, not by any means. But I was not to discover those truths until I went to live in New Zealand as a permanent resident, and began my researches there, as the rivers he wrote about were virtually on my doorstep, and the more certain and exact truth about the world's best-ever fisherman gradually emerged.

So, for the purposes of this briefer tale, it must be remembered that at that time I first approached Medford, Rogue River, and Grants Pass, with something akin to awe and veneration, as if to a holy of holies, a shrine to the wonders of fly-fishing. Until that time all I really knew of it was from Zane Grey's own account of the place, the river, the fish, and the fishing.

Even the river towns were no more than names to me: Medford, Grants Pass, and later, Gold Beach. In those days I was unaware of Ben Hur Lampman and the marvellously mellifluous words he had penned at Gold Beach into what would soon become *A Leaf from French Eddy*, the very finest of all fishing books of all time. So do we extol the Zane Greys of this world while shutting our eyes and minds to fishermen and writers like Lampman. As far as my hosts were concerned, their chief interest lay in the availability of motel accommodation and the desirability or otherwise of places to eat. It did not matter to me that, at the very best, I would see but a small part of the river and have only brief and little chance to fish its fabled waters. As I've said, this was a token visit; a symbolic journey, an early pilgrimage of sorts. It was enough simply to be there.

Between Grants Pass and Gold Beach on the coast the Rogue cuts through the Coast Range, turbulent and wild, through steep gorge country. When Zane Grey first fell under the spell of the river in the early 1920s he enjoyed what was to become a typical baptism of defeat in his steelhead fishing. Not a single one of the dozens of hooked steelhead was ever landed. His tales of those early days are full of broken lines, broken rods – almost broken hearts – as big steelhead jumped once hooked, then took off downstream into the fastest water, and simply kept on going. Grey, of course, despite his legendary fame, positively enjoyed initial defeat. It gave him the real incentive to go away, lick his wounds, plan a further "expedition" back to the river of dreams, and return as the victor, 'bringing the fish to heel,' as said by Trey Combs, 'as he had done to countless denizens on a dozen seas. Yet,' he added, 'realities have a way of tempering such grandeur, even to as formidable an angling personage as Zane Grey.'

Ironically, it was the chance reading of that remark, written after Trey Combs had made considerable researches into Grey's days on the Rogue and Umpqua, and the nature of the man himself, that crystallised in my mind a hundred different and often disparate things I had read and heard about Zane Grey's fishing in New Zealand, especially the trout fishing. Then the man himself, warts and all, began to emerge.

Of that first, unsuccessful visit by Zane Grey to the Rogue, Trey Combs wrote: 'Author and river met a short time later with the river getting the best of it; not a single steelhead was caught. When accomplishments are many and failures so few, the refusal of the Rogue to do his bidding must have affected him deeply. He gathered from the challenge a lasting love for the river. True, the heroic hyperbole so characteristic of his writing found its place here too, though with an underlying feeling of serenity without the primitive gut-fight abrasiveness seen in his duels with billfish, tuna and tarpon. These were fish fought to a standstill or lost. They took the bait or did not, and the choice lay more with the vagaries of contributing tangibles: movement of boat and movement of fish with Grey an interested third party until the fish was hooked. During the mortal test, where a bending of wills determined the outcome, Grey excelled. He had heart enough for ten. But one does not fish for steelhead in this light. The river is fished and the fish its reward. It was the Rogue that must bend Grey to its will if he was to succeed. The successes he eventually realised were most satisfying; he came back again and again – while some great fishing grounds saw his presence for but a fleeting trial.'

Grey – ever with a quite ordinary fishing trip being an "expedition"– wanted to see the Rogue in the gorge country of the Coastal Range between Grants Pass and Gold Beach. He had heard vague stories of fantastic steelhead fishing in this little known and rarely visited region. Grey and his entire fish-

175

ing party floated down the river in a small fleet of Mackenzie boats. On the downstream float they came to an open clearing and met a prospector who owned land and lived in a riverside cabin. Immediately opposite the cabin they fished through a most productive drift. In typical Grey grandiose manner, he bought the land and the cabin right there and then, on the spot. A grander house was built at Winkle Bar, and here Zane Grey made his second home – perhaps the place he best liked to be. He still wandered the world: in fact, at that time, he had not yet visited New Zealand. But he always returned to Winkle Bar on the Rogue River and here, in the most curious circumstances ever to surround the death of a fisherman, he died in 1939.

On the verandah of the house at Winkle Bar, overlooking that first, great, productive steelhead drift, Grey had built a strange contraption: a deepsea fisherman's fighting chair, bolted to the deck, swivel-mounted like the real thing. An enormous big-game rod and reel and line was connected up to an arrangement of suspended heavy weights and pulleys beneath the verandah deck. There he would sit, strapped into his deep-sea fighting chair, harnessed up to his latest billfish rod, pumping away against the suspended weights, fighting an imaginary battle with some imaginary but giant fish in some equally imaginary ocean.

By September 1939 the world was gearing up for another war. Zane Grey's long ascendant star was in decline. His western dime novels still sold in their millions of copies, but sales were still dropping. Readers, publishers, critics, kings and queens and presidents, and the rich and powerful people of the world, had had enough of Zane Grey and his bombast, petulance and arrogance. Ernest Hemingway had just declined Grey's invitation – and challenge – to accompany him on the greatest world-wide fishing junket ever known: to the most fabled oceans, seas, lakes and rivers on earth, where Grey and Hemingway would do battle and compete to prove once and for all which of them was the supreme and most famous fishing champion the world had ever known. The two men had never even met. And never did. Hemingway's star was in its ascendancy. He was far too wise and cunning to attach himself to a star in terminal decline.

There, on the front porch at Winkle Bar, strapped into his fighting chair, Grey trained during hot summer days, dreaming of yet more world records in still uncharted, unfished waters, pumping away at a grotesque paraphernalia of pulleys and weights, probably not even looking at the Rogue River right in front of him, because he was lost within an impossible and meaningless dream. Fighting that imaginary giant fish, while planning yet another great "expedition", he pumped once too much, and his heart gave out and he died.

If there were any persisting memories of Zane Grey in Medford or Grants Pass I did not see them, but then I was a guest of non-fishers and was neither able to, nor even then motivated to have delved deeper, had I been on my own. As for the towns themselves, they were less a surprise to me then, on that first visit, than they proved to be in my subsequent reading. I had been anticipating small, quaint, unspoiled riverside villages – expecting them to be rather like, say, Turangi on the banks of New Zealand's Tongariro River – but Medford was a heavily industrialised town with little to commend it. A line of tacky motels, typical of such a vast recreational area, did nothing to add to the charm. Additionally, my host's guide book stated, categorically if not with full praise: 'If you've been contemplating a fast, Medford is the place to start it.' At first sight it seemed to have all the drawbacks of a sprawling urban city, with none of the advantages.

In deference to me and to the Rogue River we drove on by Medford to the eponymous town of Rogue River itself. It was only long afterwards, back with my books, and by the time Trey Combs' books were published, that I began to wonder whether there may have been memories, or even ghosts, of Bill Isaacks, 'Toggery Bill' of Medford, and doyen of the Rogue River fishermen and more of a caretaker of the river in its heyday than Zane Grey had ever been.

The town of Rogue River is built in an idyllic location in the shimmering Rogue River Valley. Much to our surprise the town was thronged with holiday-makers, and it was plain to see that none of them were there for the once fabulous fishing. This was middle America on vacation. Zane Grey was still nowhere in sight. In fact, twenty years would pass before I read George Reiger's words that Grey, more than any man, turned wilderness America into campground chains for middle Americans. He was one of the first tourists of the wilderness, and he wrote enthusiastically about its wonders, urging his readers to go out to see and do what he had seen and done. They did.

What I didn't know then, but learned in my researches into Zane Grey's fishing "expeditions" to New Zealand, was that he had always been a tourist. The ZG trail is best followed in the pages of his books.

We drove on to Grants Pass. Although it was planned that our return journey to San Francisco would be via the coastal route on the seaward side of the mountain range, it had long been apparent that Route 5, the great North-South Expressway, was no way to see this country for the first time. While the road itself was magnificent, it trivialised the journey by trivialising nature, especially the journey I thought it would be.

Grants Pass is at the junction of this freeway and US 199, the way we should have approached it by from the coast road. I knew that from Grants Pass to Gold Beach the Rogue was reputed to be a torrent whitewater river, so my token fishing in the famed river would have to be in some more accessible reach on account of my hosts, whom I suspected were already hankering for the more cosmopolitan delights of the San Francisco Bay area. We headed back east towards Rogue River, then took a back road that more by luck than judgement brought us close by the river itself, and accessible down a steep gravelly bank.

There was something comical, almost ludicrous, with husband and wife hosts, both non-fishers, but eager that I should fish, fussing around me as I set up my fly rod. I tied on a New Zealand Red Setter – as good a fly as any I know on a strange water and perhaps a fishless one – slid down the rocky bank and cast and cast towards the setting sun.

It was probably not a good idea to have fished at all. I cast out across and slightly downstream, through as likely a run as any I saw, letting the line sink as best it could on its downstream search. It was a timeless and almost other-worldly fishing experience, although I was only eager to pack up, give up, so that my friends and hosts could get on with our journey.

I caught no fresh-run steelhead, straight in from the Pacific. Not even a good pull from a respectably sized fish. But once, on the slow retrieve, I felt a slight tug, as if a small submerged drowned twig had been snagged, and stripped in line in order to free it. But there, fully lip-hooked on the #10 Red Setter, was a gorgeously arrayed rainbow parr of about six ounces, wriggling and protesting wildly against being yanked unceremoniously from the water. I stooped to release the young fish, holding it up into the stream. It gave a final shake and shot off into the low summer water, seeming angry with me rather than relieved to be released.

I climbed up the slope towards the road where my friends were waiting. At least I had caught a trout in Zane Grey's Rogue River, and on my Hardy "Rogue River" fly rod, albeit that it was big and heavy enough to have landed a twenty-pound salmon. At that time it was enough.

We drove back towards Grants Pass and found a comfortable motel on the road to Rogue River with tree-shaded grounds leading down to the river. I think my friends were pleased to find it, for I suspect they had found the entire latter part of the day to be an exhausting and almost wilderness fishing trip! There was a good nearby restaurant. My friends were beginning to enjoy their country jaunt, and I've sometimes wondered whether afterwards, perhaps even years later, they spoke of it as having been a wilderness experience. By that time, in America, the word "wilderness" was beginning to become fashionable, appropriate to lob into dinner party, cocktail party company, indicating a new awareness and concern for matters ecological and the new spirit of the age.

Writing this now, in recollection, years after the event, I regret I did not then know as much about the Rogue River and the men who fished there as has subsequently come to my knowledge. As a tourist guest of husband and wife San Franciscans, neither of whom had any interest in fishing, it was not possible for me to do as I wished. Medford, where I would have liked to have nosed around at my leisure, was to them just another American town, much like any other, with little to offer. Just another stop for food, petrol, and overnight accommodation along the way to somewhere else.

Next day we explored the northern branch of the river along Highway 62, the road to Prospect and Crater Lake, where once again I repeated the ten minutes of a few token casts now firmly established in my hosts' minds as being a day's fishing. But, once again, there were no ghosts from the past along the Rogue – not at least as far as I was concerned – it was still just another American river.

But it did have ample compensation. The road winds through magnificent forests and meadowlands. It seemed a thousand miles away from Interstate 5. Crater Lake itself, the focal point of Oregon's only national park, is a caldera with a surface area of over 20 square miles, formed when Mount Mazama, a 15,000-feet high volcano, literally blew its top. Great cliffs and screes up to 2000 feet above water level, enfold the 6000-feet-elevation lake. The water is the most intense blue, made to seem even moreso framed as it is by the sheer stark lava cliffs. Almost 2000 feet deep and fed by melting snows, I remembered that Zane Grey had always stated that the lake was the source of the Rogue River, although this is unlikely as there is no apparent outlet. In the pseudo-animist manner he affected Zane Grey laid much emphasis on the source of things, origins and myths, yet he conspicuously declined to go to real source material, or learn anything about it, in almost everything he did. During his first visit to New Zealand he stayed overnight in Rotorua and attended a regular, scheduled, programmed Maori concert party. These were always popular and essential along the tourist trail, long before Grey's visit and continue to this day. Lasting about an hour and of dubious cultural authenticity, they are entertaining, well worth the cost, and simply meant as entertainment. Embroidering the event, a month later, when writing *The Angler's Eldorado: New Zealand* on the return voyage to the United States by scheduled passenger liner, it had become "I spent some time living among the Maori tribes of New Zealand." The fact is, he seems to have been no different in his travels around the United States, or anywhere else for that matter.

Grey, of course, fished in Crater Lake on his first visit to the Pacific Northwest. Despite the fact that great changes had taken place in the ensuing forty years, Crater Lake was a tourist resort then as, indeed, it still is to this day. But in the same way in which Zane Grey always suggested that his fishing "expeditions" to New Zealand were into previously unexplored and unknown wilderness mountain fastness rivers (whereas, in fact, his "camp" on the banks of the Tongariro River had been built by the government a few months earlier to accommodate the Duke and Duchess of York, afterwards King George VI and his wife, the present Queen Elizabeth the Queen Mother, then on a state visit to New Zealand), so similarly did he make his visit to Crater Lake seem to be to the far ends of the earth:

> That walk, or rather climb, was pleasant despite
> its difficulties. Giant brown-barked fir trees stood
> majestically out of the snowdrifts, and their soft
> green foliage shone beautifully against the back-
> ground of white. The fragrance of these great
> Oregon pines was so cold and sweet. Mrs Grey and

I rather lagged behind my brother and the rest of
the party. The altitude was hard on my wife, not to
mention the steep parts of the icy trail. We rested a
good many times and profited by that in our enjoy-
ment of the white-and-green forest, and the occasional glimpse through the timber out over the wild
range. Towards the summit, where the ascent grew
steeper, we were hard put to it to make headway.
Mrs Grey is wonderfully mathematical, and she said
often, between panting breaths, "If we – slip back –
two steps – for almost – every step up – when shall
we – get there?"

Finally we reached level ground from which the
snow had melted. Evidently there was a considerable strip of this ground between where we stood
and the rim of the crater. I could not see the lake.
To our right a jagged range of snowy rock rose high
and appeared to circle away toward the north. To
our left bare ground and green grass led up to a
stone house which evidently was a hotel.

Crossing this strip, we soon stood upon the rim,
with Crater Lake far beneath us.

To this day the tourist guide books give Crater Lake full
praise when it comes to its natural beauty and are free with
adjectival excesses, but none so like Zane Grey, who continued:

I expected something remarkable, but was not prepared for a scene of such wonder and beauty.
Crater Lake was a large body of water set down
deep in a pit of an extinct volcano. It seemed a blue
gulf. Nowhere else had I ever seen such a shade of
blue. This color was not azure blue or sea blue.
How exquisite, rare, unreal! After a moment I
seemed to think that it resembled the blue of heaven
seen from the peak of a high mountain. This rare

blue is not of the earth. Crater Lake had more similarity to an amethyst than any jewel I knew. An amethyst in which tints of lavender and heliotrope were dominated by blue! The colour, then, of this wonderful lake was its most striking feature.

Here in the telling of his tale Zane Grey might more typically have gone off into the woods and found "an old Indian, steeped in the lore of the region," who would have put him on to the choicest fishing spots. That would have best suited the pseudo-animist in Grey (who sometimes claimed to have Indian blood in his veins, but almost certainly didn't), but he went on to say that although there were plenty of tourists at the nearby campsite, none could speak English. But as he could not find a convenient Indian chief to give him the true gen, he did find a "workman" who was able to tell of the giant tackle-busting lunker trout inhabiting the depths of the lake.

After adventures avoiding bears, Grey got into the fishing. Lunkers all, they came to his fly, but the rainbow trout they caught were in such poor condition he opined that Crater Lake was no place for them. But it still had to be adventure:

Climbing out was hard, because it was almost straight up and we were burdened by the weight of the fish. But we took our time and rested every few steps. I certainly enjoyed the ascent more than the descent. I had leisure to look about me. A breeze had rippled and ruffled the surface of the lake, somehow marvellously transforming the colour of the water. Great white clouds sailed in the sky and were reflected in the lake. The wind sang in the fir trees. I did not see a bird or an animal of any species.

When we reached the danger zone where it was necessary to cross and climb, we found that the softened snow made safe travel. We did not care how

183

laborious it was. We were nearly two hours in climbing out, part of which time, of course, we had rested. On the whole it was an adventure well worth experiencing. The kingdom of adventure is within us. A trip or a fishing jaunt or a climb upon the hills is successful and happy only as we possess in our hearts the things we go out to seek.

I rested and lingered on the rim of the Crater Lake long after the others had started down towards camp. I seemed to wait for something I had not yet gained . . . .

We can perhaps get somewhere closer to an understanding of Zane Grey's metaphysical ponderings when we realize that his "expedition" approaching Crater Lake consisted of automobiles carrying Grey and his family, his brother, the ever-present Captain Mitchell, numerous friends and hangers-on, secretaries, cooks, stewards, professional fishermen, photographers; trucks carrying enormous quantities of stores and provisions – and that in all probability Grey and his wife walked up the last few hundred yards in order to make what he would have considered a more fitting and appropriate arrival of the great outdoorsman – at the hotel!

Forty years on and barely four weeks on into the summer from the time of Grey's arrival, Chris and his wife Anne, and I, drove right up to that same hotel without seeing a single snowflake or bear, and enjoyed a remarkably civilised lunch. Afterwards I didn't have the heart to suggest I go fishing.

We returned to Medford via a scenic mountain road around Klamath Falls and lake. This was all more to my hosts' idea of what they had hoped to find. But they were still determined that I should see the mouth of the Rogue River, where it entered the Pacific.

There was no direct road from Grants Pass to Gold Beach, so next day we set off on the big sweep south and back into California to Smith River, before turning north again on the

184

Pacific coast road. Here were thick stands of redwood and Douglas fir with the fog rolling in from the sea.

Even in those days I should have known better than to believe Zane Grey. Gold Beach was far from being the site of a primitive riverside fishing camp. More than anything, I suppose, I was astonished at the size of the towns we passed through. Somehow I had expected tiny rural hamlets, but everything hereabouts was geared up to twentieth century American vacationing. Maybe it was inevitable. Maybe it happens everywhere. Yet, only a few years later, did I begin to realise that wherever Zane Grey went, he described it as having been a rugged backwoods experience, whereas it hadn't been like that even at the time of Zane Grey's visitations. It just suited him better to say so.

He made that first whitewater boat journey down the Rogue from Grants Pass to Gold Beach sound to have been a unique pioneering adventure and exploration. As usual the entire ZG "expedition" made it: brother, son, odd friends, his Japanese cook, the ubiquitous Englishman, Captain Laurie Mitchell, and sundry others. It was no doubt an exciting and invigorating journey, with some good fishing on the way; and it was here that Grey first saw Winkle Bar.

There was a certain naivety in Zane Grey's writing when he let slip certain facts that belied the tales he told. After filling the better part of *Tales of Fresh-Water Fishing* with adulatory accounts of the Rogue, all of which made it seem to have been a first-ever expedition into a hitherto unexplored wilderness, he bemoans that "the authorities above Grants Pass opened the gates of the irrigation dam and let a flood of muddy water down to defile the clear waters of the Rogue." Then, whilst still telling the unexplored wilderness tale, he can add " . . . I expected to find the Rogue, after we left Alameda, twenty miles below Grants Pass, to be one of the wildest, purest, and most beautiful of all rivers. It was certainly one of the most beautiful, but the other attributes failed. Miners, prospectors, halfbreed Indians, and a few whites scattered down the valley, effectively kill any suggestion of utter solitude. There were wild stretches of the river, to be sure, but just when you imagined you were drifting into an untrodden wilderness then your dream would be dispelled."

True to form, however, the very next paragraph is back into the untamed wilderness, as if the previous sentences had never been written. Even granting that things were more primitive thereabouts in 1925 than they are today, it is fairly safe to assume that the miners, prospectors, halfbreed Indians and sundry whites he encountered on the trip were less pioneering folk than he cared to admit. It was just Zane Grey being Zane Grey, creating the myth, establishing the legend.

A more truthful picture of the Rogue was painted by Trey Combs in his fine book *Steelhead fly-fishing & Flies*. And most of his catalogue of fabled Rogue River anglers had been long established there long before Zane Grey ever saw the place:

> . . . The Rogue was a float through solitude, an adventure, and anglers found in the experience many reasons to settle more or less permanently on the river. The character of its steelhead, a race more attracted to the fly than any other, helped invite this decision.
>
> The dwellings could be rustic seasonal cabins or palatial homes. Their owners were envied, and as they fished they became part of the Rogue's folklore. Among the best known Rogue residents were Fred Noyes (a millionaire, some say), Fred Burnham (then, as now, a legend), Frank Madison, Andrew Welch, Nion Tucker, Cappy Black, Bill Isaacks and Zane Grey. Their many friends who joined them each season numbered in the hundreds. A few must be mentioned for many readers will endearingly recognise them as part of their own – and steelheading's – most memorable past: Brownie and Cox Webb, Rainbow Gibson, Al Cook, Charley

Adair, C. A. Swope, H. H. Pringle, Al Knudson, J. P. Cuenen, Ivan Kesterton, Benjamin Hart, D. G. McNeil, Auston Brownell, M. N. Hogan, Bill Haywood, Paul Shearer, Bruce Holding, John Dose, Ed Lamport and Joe Wharton.

Bill Isaacks epitomised the resident's devotion for the Rogue River. He lived all his adult life in Medford and became one of its leading citizens. As owner of the Toggery menswear store, he became known as "Toggery Bill". He sought to bring culture to Medford and many famous singers and musicians entertained in the community. But Isaacks was above all else a remarkably skilled steelhead fly-fisherman, kindly giving technical advice, recommending patterns and disclosing favourite runs. He fished Leonard and Parker rods, Hardy reels, lines and leaders, tackle purchased at Lamport's Sporting Goods, for Ed Lamport stocked the finest English and domestic fly tackle in Medford.

When President Herbert Hoover travelled west to fish the Rogue, he did so as the guest of Toggery Bill, the two, and the presidential entourage, staying at Isaack's handsome log cabin. Reporters, photographers and the naturally curious denied the couple solitude, and Hoover was given to testily remark: "By the attendance of the fishing party, I would judge the country is predominantly Republican, but I wish that they would give me room enough to cast a fly. I would hate to hook a good Republican by the seat of his pants."

Isaacks fished from Curry Riffle to Three River Riffle with his favourite, Grapevine Riffle, beginning a half-mile below his cabin. On this small part of the Rogue he cast his fly and will be remembered because he fished it so well and cared for his Rogue and her steelhead and his companions equally.

187

If Bill Isaacks symbolised the caretaker's love for the Rogue, Zane Grey exemplified the powerful, wealthy and dedicated visiting angler. If Grey wasn't loved or even respected on the Rogue, there is no doubt he was held in awe. He was more force than man, a giant personality famous for his many books of cowboy fiction and autobiographical accounts of fishing adventures. His fertile mind and great energy produced dozens of books that gained an astonishing following. Though he dearly loved this river, I question whether he was ever at peace with it or its people. He sought to overcome the Rogue, to subject its steelhead to the force of his efforts, thus attempting to thrash them accordingly. His was an entourage of flattering followers. He hired guides and non-guides to safeguard favorite riffles. They took dawn stations before the holding water he would later fish at his leisure. Anglers encountering these human obstructions called them "thugs" for the meetings were anything but pleasant.

Unfortunately Trey Combs' book was not published until 1976. Ironically, I first read the book, immediately on publication, on a subsequent visit to Oregon. As to the Zane Grey version of events, one might be forgiven for thinking that Grey came to the Rogue a few generations before Isaacks and President Hoover and the rest. They were, in fact, more or less contemporary occurrences.

※　※　※　※　※

There seems little more to say other than by way of postscript. Since then the upper river has been dammed, the abuse of the Rogue was not confined to the rapacious salmon fishery. A more recent observer spoke of the denudation of the coastal mountains, and from shortage of water and the

188

impediments of irrigation dams in the upper reaches. Continuing with yet more anger, Anthony Netboy wrote: "The Corps of Engineers in its empire-building mania has fastened on the upper Rogue and is blockading the main stem at Lost Creek and impounding the tributary Elk Creek. It also plans to dam the Applegate River, a bucolic tributary of the Rogue. These projects, which will cost the American taxpayer $200 million, are of doubtful value, though sold to the Congress mainly as flood control, recreation, and fishery enhancement undertakings. They have been promoted primarily by land speculators and politicians eager for 'pork barrel' benefits. The new hatchery that was used to gain approval of the dams from such organisations as the Izaak Walton League, National Wildlife Federation, and anglers generally will produce salmon to restock the river. Thus another whitewater river will be lost to posterity."

It would be wrong, however, to suppose that these degradations suffered by the Rogue are either all of relatively recent origin or caused by the Corps of Engineers in their bureaucratic fervour to build dams and meddle with the natural state of perfectly good rivers. The degradation began long before Zane Grey discovered the Rogue.

The Indian tribes to whom the land and rivers belonged were Athabascan-speaking peoples. They were skilled fishermen and wood-carvers, who made war canoes that could carry up to sixty men out to sea, excellent bows and arrows, and household utensils of cedar root fibre or tough grasses. They depended heavily on shellfish and fish for food and venerated the Salmon Spirit. In the later nineteenth century the Indians were removed from their native lands and herded into the Siletz and Grand Ronde Reservations on the coast; sometimes they did not accept this fate without a bloody war and massacres. A chief of the Rogue River Indians expressed the feelings of all the tribes during peace negotiations that ended the terrible wars of the 1850s:

This is my country; I was in it when these trees

189

were very little higher than my head. My heart is sick fighting the whites, but I want to live in my own country. I will, if the whites are willing, go back to the Deer Creek country and live as I used to among the whites; they can visit my camp and I will visit theirs; but I will not lay down my arms and go to the reserve. I will fight.

After the Indians had been expelled from their lands the whites took over. One of the first rivers to be exploited for its fisheries was the Rogue, where gold had been discovered, at Jacksonville, in 1851, and where the salmon and steelhead ran in huge numbers. The river rises in the Cascade Range northwest of Crater Lake and flows through the Klamath Mountains in a northwest course to the ocean at Gold Beach, a distance of about two hundred miles.

In 1876 R. D. Hume, who with his brothers had pioneered salmon canning on the Sacramento and Columbia Rivers, came to the Rogue looking for a new fishery to exploit. Seeing that the river was amply stocked with spring and autumn chinook, he purchased an existing saltery and lumber mill that went with it and began to buy land on both banks. Eventually he owned a stretch of twelve miles from the mouth of the river upstream, thus acquiring a virtual monopoly on the fishery. Besides a stationary trap, he used set nets in the spring and a 750-foot seine in the autumn to harvest the salmon.

In 1877 Hume built a small hatchery that was later enlarged and improved. He was in fact the first private individual to undertake artificial propagation of salmon on the Pacific coast. From 1880 to 1900 he packed an average of 16,000 cases annually. He also operated a saltery that packed over 500 barrels yearly, each weighing 200 pounds. Hume was probably the first Oregon canner to break into the English market. At the turn of the century the Liverpool firm of Pelling & Stanley was importing 250,000 cans of Oregon salmon yearly, almost all from Hume. Anthony Netboy commented:

Hume dabbled in mining, sawmilling, and other ventures and by the end of the century, when he was elected to the state legislature, was a millionaire. Called the 'Salmon King of Oregon,' he was arrogant, combative, and litigious, defying the law and the courts when they interfered with his strong moneymaking proclivities. He must be credited, however, with some foresight, because he realised that the Rogue River could not indefinitely support his intensive kind of fishing. He was convinced that restocking the river with fish from his hatchery was partly responsible for his large packs (a doubtful assumption) and maintained that the catches fell off when no hatchery work was done. In 1893 he published a treatise on artificial propagation that described his methods, rather crude by modern standards. This, however, was a pioneer effort.

Hume castigated the packers for their failure to support salmon culture and fishery conservation (which of course he did not practice). He predicted that "unless such steps are taken, in less than ten years the packing of salmon on the Columbia River will have become impossible as a business proposition." His forecast was only off by a few decades, for in the 1950s the salmon canning business ended on the Oregon coast and had not long to go on the Columbia.

For salmon canners like Hume the steelhead trout was of no importance whatsoever. Today the Rogue is a designated sport fishery, with chinook salmon and steelhead trout the main quarry. Anthony Netboy recorded that some 20,000 salmon are landed annually in the 200-mile Rogue and up to 10,000 steelhead trout. Below Grants Pass it is a sanctuary scenic river, but above this it is, in Netboy's words, "a dreary reservoir behind the Corps of Engineers' Lost Creek dam."

❊ ❊ ❊ ❊ ❊

At least I had cast a fly into the tumbling waters of the Rogue. I had even caught a six ounce rainbow. As I have long advocated that splendid motto of the Flyfishers' Club, Piscator non solum piscatur – There is more to fishing than catching fish – I cannot complain!

❊ ❊ ❊ ❊ ❊

As fishing trips go it had been disappointing, a non- event, to say the least. But then, it was never meant to be a fishing trip in the first place: more a chasing of a willo' the wisp; not even a spectre. It was probably more to do with my Hardy split cane "Rogue River" fly rod than I realised. If I did not find there on the Rogue even a semblance of Zane Grey's ghost – albeit he died overlooking its banks – it was either because he'd never really been there, in the first place, at least not in the way that Bill Isaacks had been there, or because he had died strapped into that ridiculous, nonsensical contraption of a deepsea fighting chair with his mind, as always, on an impossible dream of somewhere else.

What was to stem from that pilgrimage of sorts to the Rogue materialised twenty years afterwards when, living in New Zealand, I began my long researches into Zane Grey's fishing and fishing "expeditions" in New Zealand. Even then, fifty years after Grey's visits, his name – both as a man and as a fisherman – was much revered in New Zealand. His own self-publicity and plain duplicity, as well as his own remark-able charisma, had endowed his memory with the halo of near sainthood.

But as I re-read his books, studied the government and other archives for correspondence and memos, talked to people, walked and fished the same rivers where he and his comic-

192

opera entourage supposedly camped and fished, I was already with more factual knowledge of the same man as he had been on the Rogue, and how he had behaved there, and how he had been seen. He was no different in New Zealand, except that he went there with the government's blessing and considerable assistance, and that they, too, contributed to this myth of saint-hood. As for that first strange visit of mine to the Rogue River, I now know – but there was no way of knowing then – that I had been chasing the wrong willo' the wisp.

❋ ❋ ❋ ❋ ❋

During those few days we passed up and down the Medford- Rogue River road through Gold Hill so many times in our comings and goings that it became vaguely familiar. It would be several years before – with maturing attitudes to fly-fishing – I became aware of Ben Hur Lampman, whose book, *A Leaf from French Eddy*, is perhaps the most perfect book about fishing since Walton. It was first published, posthumously, in 1965, and was as little known then as it is to this day, although a new edition of the book appeared in 1979: it, too, disappear-ing where many such good books go to die.

Lampman's origins were in the flatlands of North Dakota and the lake country of Wisconsin where he caught his first fish. In Vernon Hidy's Introduction to the book he tells that Lampman "married a vibrant, adventuresome school teacher from upstate New York and together they travelled West into the mountainous grandeur of Oregon where he started his career as a fisherman-printer-writer":

> They settled on the banks of the Rogue River and he printed a weekly newspaper called *The Gold Hill News*. Here, from 1912 to 1916, the lyric Lampman prose first attracted attention and the natives coined a name for him: The Oracle of Gold Hill. Then his competence as a writer took him to Portland where

193

he specialized in polished editorials and nature
essays for a daily newspaper . . .   . . . In these pages
you will find the vintage prose, the humour and the
sentiments which prompt many men to salute Ben
Hur Lampman once or more each season with a
glass or cup of spirits beside the very waters he
fished and wrote about with remarkable luck.
Moreover, if you are one of those who have been
soothed by the music of rivers and the magic of
lakes, one of those who have a reverence for the
fish, trees and wildlife such waters sustain, this will
be a special book for you. Parts of it are mysteri-
ously haunting . . . inspired phrases and mellow
insights such as Coleridge had in mind when he
observed that musical writing, with true rhythm and
melody in the words, usually possesses something
deep and good in the meaning too.

So Lampman lived and fished on the banks of the Rogue
River – long before Zane Grey had even heard of the place,
and in a highly civilised cultured fashion that makes a mock-
ery of Grey's "expeditions" into wild, unexplored territories.
Despite that tinkling alliterative name "Rogue River" that
trips off the tongue and suggests much to any fisherman,
Lampman never once actually names the river throughout his
book. In fact he writes as if he is writing about rivers everywhere, rather than the Rogue in particular:

Now, angling for the silver-flanked trout is well
enough, in its way; indeed, it is such angling as can
have no superior, whether in saltwater or in fresh.
But the angler dissembles somewhat when he gives
it as his opinion that he, and others of his fraternity,
are catching trout and nothing else, unless   it be a
whitefish or so, or possibly a chub. This conclusion
is not susceptible of serious argument when it is

agreed that these same trout, tamed and held in an
ugly pool of angular concrete, would not and could
not arouse the enthusiasm of anglers, or kindle their
eyes with unaccustomed brightness. It is true that
an angler might deign to angle in such a pool as is
described, but his heart would not be there, and a
cynic shadow would rest upon his countenance. He
would do so, if, indeed he yielded, for the sufficient
reason that no wilder water was near at hand or
lawfully available. You must remember that in this
frequent praise of Isaak Walton, whose memory is
as green as a willow in Devon – and properly so – we
have more or less forgotten another angler, who was
Simon called Simple. Ah, there was the personifica-
tion of the inward angler, or the driven fisherman!
Of the fisherman who must fish! Of perennial and
patient optimism! But we set out to prove that sans
the setting the delights of angling would be negligi-
ble and antic. And this, it now appears, requires no
further demonstration. For they who angle for silver-flanked trout, and who will penetrate the
blessed wilderness this day, shall catch the golden
mimulus where it grows in the cold clay of the riverbank, and the picket-fence rattle of the belted kingfisher flashing by, and an odour of fern, and the roar
and shouting of waters, and laughter, and that far
sound that is the wraith of a sound – the reiterant
bell-like music of silence in the forest. True, if fortune favours them they will catch fish also, and lose
fish too, and boast mightily of their adventuring and
their cleverness. But the weight of the laden creel at
evening is not the worth of the outing, and well they
know it. Nevertheless, be chary of how you suggest
these other matters to them, for they are pleased to
think they are practical fellows, and sinewy sports-
men, as red-blooded as the hero of a book by Zane

Grey. If they turn upon you with profanity, please remember at least that you were forewarned. Good fishing!

So Lampman, who never mentioned the name Rogue River, yet lived on its banks and fished there, and only once mentioned Zane Grey obliquely, not as a fellow fisherman, or as a nearby neighbour, but as the best-selling author of purple prose dime westerns with pure and sinewy heroes, sets the background for his tales of fishing. Lampman was ten years younger than Grey, but was already writing, printing, and publishing *The Gold Hill News* and living beside and fishing the Rogue River when Zane Grey first came there in the early 1920s. They would have been there at the same time. Yet they lived in two very different worlds.

For Lampman going fishing was an event to be savoured to the full. For Grey it was always and exactly like Robert Davis once said of him, that if Zane went out with a mosquito net to catch minnows, he would make it sound like a Roman gladiator setting forth to slay whales in the Tiber.

When I went briefly to the Rogue I had been looking for the wrong man. I should have been looking for Ben Hur Lampman. With a little bit of luck I might even have brought away a leaf from French Eddy. I would have liked that.

❆　❆　❆　❆　❆

I have never gone back to the Rogue River, not because I did not wish to do so, but rather because the chance never arose again, and there are so many other rivers in the world. After that first odd visit we made our way back to San Francisco along the coast road, past rivers even more fabled than the Rogue. The summer fog was with us all the way, rolling in from the Pacific, cold and damp to the touch.

The Golden Gate Bridge was wreathed in fog and sunshine, together, as only happens there, as we crossed into that most delightful city. We stopped for dinner at Fisherman's Wharf. If I remember rightly we all ate chinook salmon, and very good it was, too.

WHAKAMOENGA: THE SECRET PLACE

There are many strange stories told by the Maori people of Taupo in connection with the Tongariro group (Ruapehu, Ngauruhoe and Tongariro) which they regard as their Sacred Mountain. They tell of the loves and of the battles of this great mountain, of the priestly ceremonies and adventures of Ngatoroirangi, and of the multitudes of demons and genii that lived on its rocky heights.

It is said that the three volcano-peaks of this sacred mountain were haunted by supernatural beings who had as their chiefs, Te Ririo, Takaka, and Taunapiki. The three chiefs were the guardians of the mountain and visited those who infringed the tapu. They were visible only when they came to punish those who violated the stringent laws. The offenders, we are told, were sometimes seized and carried off into enchanted regions; sometimes they were merely killed; at other times they were left for years under a kind of spell.

John Te Heu Heu Grace, Tuwharetoa

The war party approached Taupo from the direction of Mangakino and came out at Waihaha. It journeyed to Rangatira Point and there came across

Tuwharetoa a Turiroa and his wife Hineteao living at
Ponui. This was a stronghold and situated on the
steep, cliffy mound on the eastern side of the point.
It has long since been deserted and overgrown with
fern, but the scarped walls and trenches can still be
traced. Hineteao was captured and killed. Her husband escaped and ran along the eastern shore of the
lake to Whakaangiangi Pa. He informed Te Rangiita
and Tumatangaua of what had happened and warned
them of Te Atainutai's approach.

ibid

All fly-fishermen need a secret place they can call their own.
It need not be a place they own in the more prosaic sense
of ownership, any more than it need be a place known to them
alone, where no other angler ever casts a fly. I once had such a
place, and of it I shall now sing praise.

With a fly rod in hand it has always been my preference to
be astream wading a trout river, ever probing upstream,
searching out the likely and the not so likely places for a feeding brown or rainbow. Best of all this is done in summer, wading through a clear mountain stream, unhindered by the bulk
and insularity of clumsy waders. Instead, my further preference is for those warmer days when one can wade deep as
needs be in stout wading boots and stockings, and ordinary
cotton twill trousers in place of a dulling enclosure in thick
rubber or neoprene. With the chill – but not too chill – of a
summer stream climbing cooly, wetly, up one's legs is to be in
contact with the water and the trout in ways denied by thigh or
chest waders. For me, such is the acme of fly-fishing.

But my secret place is not such a place. Instead, it is a place
where one can fish dryshod; where, in fact, it is not only better
but safer, too, to fish whilst wearing almost any ordinary casu-
al outdoor footwear. Some fortunate anglers may live right
alongside a delectable trout stream, but when all is said and

done, they are not only favoured but few and far between, and possibly spoiled. Most fly-fishermen have to travel some distance to get to their fishing, and I have often journeyed hundreds of miles to get to mine. But once I had it on my doorstep.

Always preferring stream fishing to stillwaters I have nonetheless often derived great joy from fishing lakes, lagoons, and other such open impoundments of water, indeed as many of these present tales tell. But when I went to live close by the shores of Lake Taupo I doubted whether I would ever fish in the great lake itself – always preferring one of the countless streams running into it. Instead, within a year or two I only rarely fished the Tongariro River or the Hinemaiaia, the Waihaha or the Tauranga-Taupo, rather travelling further afield to fish the mountain streams of other adjoining watersheds beyond the Taupo basin.

But I did become entranced by one particular place on the lakeshore itself, and so close to my home that I could be in my study, or wake up in my bed before the dawn, then decide to go fishing, and be casting a fly in seven minutes in what, to me, soon became one of the most delectable places on this earth. In eight years of living in Acacia Bay I must have gone fishing at Whakamoenga – for this was the name of my special place – hundreds of times. Yet each time was somehow special. I never arrived there without awe, and never came away without due and proper thankfulness.

But first, the setting, because most special places of the kind I mean owe much of their hold over a man in the very nature of their settings. There is something about their geography, their situation, that the only passionate Chinese fly-fisherman I've ever known would have explained in a masterful dissertation on the ancient geomancy of feng-shui. Although they become places of the mind, by which I do not mean imaginary places, but places about which one thinks a great deal; places that spark imaginative wonder, involuntarily living in them inside one's head, their vision is such best remembered and seen again in one's mind in terms of their physical surroundings: what it was like to be there.

The Maori language of New Zealand is mellifluous and poetic, linguistically precise in naming the world around them, yet resorting to the stuff of poetry whenever this naming of things and places involved ideas, thoughts, abstractions, and the myths out of which they themselves had sprung, and by which precepts they sought to live. To an English eye the word Whakamoenga looks a harsh word, and in the way he might pronounce it, would sound hard, too. First, WH – properly pronounced something like a soft sibilant Ph-sound, as in the first syllable of 'pheasant'; but softer, with a touch of a V-sound and an F-sound on top of the Ph-sound, so that the sound just slides out between not too tightly closed lips. So that the entire word slips out something like 'Phorka-mowengah', unaccented and continuous in sound.

It means 'A Place of Sleeping', but not a place for sleeping, or any old place to sleep, but a special place. Of which more later. Lake Taupo in the Maori tongue is Taupo Moana – the Sea of Taupo – and well named, too, in describing the biggest and greatest lake in all of Australasia – a continent in itself, of many lakes. Covering a surface area of 618 square kilometres or 238 square miles, the lake lies in a series of volcanic craters. Some of its statistics are awesome. The lake contains 60 cubic kilometres of pure and remarkably clear fresh water – sufficient to cover all of the North Island to a depth of half a metre. And it lies almost exactly in the very centre of the North Island.

Taupo is a deep lake; the deepest point, 164 metres down, is a hole on the south side of Horomatangi Reef. Eighty-five percent of the lake is deeper than 50 metres. The lake is fed by many rivers, including the Tongariro, Waiotaka, Waimarino, Tauranga-Taupo, Hinemaiaia, Waitahanui, Waihoro, Otupoto, Waihaha, Whanganui, Kuratau, Tokaanu, and many smaller streams. The lake is drained by the Lower Waikato River at the outlet at the town of Taupo. Rainfall on the lake catchment area amounts to some 7528 million cubic metres a year. About

32 percent of the total water returns to the atmosphere either by evaporation or by evapotranspiration from plants. The remaining 68 percent drains down the Waikato River. On average each year, 5554 million cubic metres of water pass through the lake and, since its volume is 59,097 million cubic metres, the average time a drop of water remains in the lake is 10.6 years.

Such a huge volume of fresh water acts as a huge store of heat energy. Consequently, the minimum water temperature of 10.6°C is relatively warm compared with the winter air. However, this large mass of water takes enormous quantities of solar energy to heat, and surface temperatures in summer only briefly rise above 20° C. The bottom waters of the lake are virtually constant in temperature throughout the year.

Because of its size the curvature of the earth significantly affects visibility across the lake. Anyone standing with their feet at water level can see the surface of the lake for only three nautical miles, and everything beyond that is over the horizon. The total curvature of the lake is 29.8 metres.

The sheer size of the lake creates a physical environment not usually associated with lakes. One such phenomenon is a pattern of water movement called Langmuir Circulation, first noted in the Atlantic Ocean. Lake Taupo is much affected by the upwelling of bottom waters, previously only apparent in the deepest oceans.

The reader, it is hoped, will forgive that little barrage of statistics, but in trying to get on with my story of Whakamoenga Point I have tried to show some background to the immensity of the place. If statistics provide the background, then the backdrop to this great and stunningly beautiful sheet of water must be the snow-capped peaks of Tongariro, Ngauruhoe, and Ruapehu far across the lake to the south, slumbering volcanoes all. Then, to the east lie the winter snow-capped peaks of the Kaimanawas, and behind the town of Taupo, just across the lake from here lies Mount Tauhara. Away to the west and clearly seen through a blue-green haze of light are the fabled Western Bays, beloved of Zane Grey.

But my tale is of Whakamoenga Point, and although it is set there, right in the middle of all this scenic splendour, its immediate environs are more contained, more manageable, more knowable.

Despite the awesome number of miles down and across the lake at its widest point to the south, here closer to the town of Taupo, is more intimacy of place. In its primeval state, long before human habitation, the rain and snow-melt waters pouring out from this great basin gouged out a smaller bay at the outlet to what is now the Waikato River that runs through the town of Taupo. It is of a nice comfortable size – a mere four miles across and long, and a lovely bay – Tapuaeharuru Bay – at the head of which stands the town, and beyond which to the south, outside the bay, lies the great open expanse of Lake Taupo itself – the Sea of Taupo.

On the western shore of Tapuaehururu Bay lies Acacia Bay, where I lived. Just two miles beyond my home, at the end of a private pumice road, with a locked gate at its end and a road of sorts leading towards a single house, generally unoccupied in those days, above Rangatira Point, a rocky outcrop beneath a cliff that faced straight out into the main body of the lake itself, looking south towards the snow-peaked volcanoes of the Tongariro National Park.

I mention the locked gate only because I was privileged to have a key to it, and to me it was sometimes like possessing a key to the kingdom of heaven. In seven minutes flat I drove from my home in Acacia Bay – and in those days I kept three or four fly rods, always made up, in my garage – then down through the sweep of the bay by the lakeshore, and out along the dusty pumice road that led to the Point – out of the car, opened the locked gate, drove in, then closed and locked it behind me, then drive the remaining few hundred yards to the open clearing near the house that led to a steep path through the thick native bush, twisting down that enchanted path to the rocky outcrop of Whakamoenga itself – and as I came out of the canopy of native bush I would unkeeper my artificial fly and begin stripping off line, false casting, so that by the time I stood on the outer end of the short spit of storm-softened volcanic rock I could release a first long cast out into the waters of the lake. In seven minutes flat from my home I could be fishing.

Not always, by any means, but often enough to keep one on one's toes with heightened expectancy, that first cast was rewarded with a fish.

A long-fingered, deeply fissured sandstone rock ran out into the lake. It faced almost directly due south. Straight out in front, in the direction of that first cast, lay almost the entire length of Lake Taupo – eighteen uninterrupted miles of water to the southern shores of the lake and, there, many miles still further south, but often so clearly visible one felt one might almost reach out and touch them, were the snow-capped peaks of the three mountains, Tongariro, Ngauruhoe, and Ruapehu.

Straight out in front where my fly line had alighted on the water, it plummeted down for fifty or sixty feet without interruption. Except when galeforce southerlies lashed and crashed over the Point, as they sometimes did, and apart from brief times of the day when the sun was not quite right, one could see through this lake water of such astounding clarity that every rock, every fissure, every patch of sand on the bottom, stood out clearly – even the patrolling rainbows gliding silently by.

In summer the vast shoals of smelt moved close inshore, and the trout – both rainbows and browns, but especially the rainbows – made feasting and marauding raids upon them. At such times the artificial fly might be taken right on top, or as it sank through the first few feet of water. Mostly, however, and for me the cream of the fishing there, it was best to use a fast-sinking line, and be very patient while the line sank downwards towards the bottom – a process that always took at least a minute longer than the most patient angler estimated. In fact, by the time the fly line sank in a great parabola, with the leader and fly behind the middle section of the line, the weight of the fly line, the angler's height (about eight or ten feet above the waterline), and the geometry of the average cast, by the time the fly itself reached the bottom it was not far out into the lake from where the angler stood. But this was an advantage, and the real technique for fishing at Whakamoenga. The smelt stayed close inshore, hugging the rocks, and the patrolling habits of the rainbows brought them close inshore hereabouts.

In this manner the retrieved fly was being twitched upwards almost vertically only a yard or two, or even close against, the almost sheer cliff-like faces of rock directly under the fisherman's position above. A patrolling trout would see the artificial fly ascending the rockface in a series of spurts, short jerks – and if it had a mind to have it, it would do so with an often savage take before turning away from the wall of rocks towards the less alien outer water.

The usual take of a good Whakamoenga rainbow often went something like this. The cast was approaching the end of the retrieve – perhaps five or six yards of fly line, plus the leader, outside the rod tip. The twitched-in fly line hanging almost vertically downwards only a foot or two outwards, laterally, from where one stood. The first indication of a strike was not a pull downwards, in line with the vertical fly line, but a sudden sensation that the underwater fly line was being carried outwards into the lake, so the forces one was aware of were at right angles to each other.

As often as not, and always with a good trout, line screamed off the reel instantaneously, always straight out across the lake, and within a second or two the hooked rainbow would leap high out of the water in a shower of spray. With miles of water around and a powerful trout, it was indeed best to let them have their heads, for you could be almost certain of being taken out well into the backing, and that there would be six, maybe ten, such runs before the fish would not still have the upper hand and be directing events.

Nevertheless, with these great Taupo rainbows it was wise to make a show of power and authority in between repeated runs, and whenever getting line back on the reel. It was near folly to try and handle them with a hand-controlled line. But even on the reel, a high-held and upright rod was always dangerously in the fish's favour. Many, many such trout break off that way. But they do respond to two tactics. The best of all is to apply gentle but firm sidestrain, then to lead the trout, like a dog on a lead, around or along the Point towards the place where one has already planned to net it – usually accomplished only be finding a place where one might clamber or slide down a rock to be able to stand close enough to guide the fish in, and slip a long-handled landing net under it. If there was no place in which to take the fish like a dog on a lead, then the second strategy was to use sidestrain only. It was remarkable how a good trout would buck and pull – and often recover and start running again – when subjected to the force applied by a rod held vertically, in a straight up arc. But with the rod lowered and held almost parallel to the water, and judicious sidestrain applied, the fish could soon be brought to the net and with far less chance of it coming off in the process.

But here I am already into fishing, and into instruction of sorts – something I promised not to do in this book, because it is not such a book, and I am neither that sort of fly-fisherman, nor competent to do so. Instead, I promised to describe some of the physical background to the place; to attempt to say something about what it was like to be there at Whakamoenga Point, as a backdrop to the fishing itself.

That, in fact, just about sums up the magic this place held for me. In perhaps hundreds of visits over a period of eight years, I never once got to the bottom of the steep path through the native bush, out on to the rocky foreshore itself, without a feeling of enormous exhilaration and well-being, without breaking into a run, to approach the water as quickly as possible, and to get my fly out there on its first cast, sinking, scintillating, flashing downwards deeply through the sunlit water, searching out a hungry, willing rainbow trout.

So there, in front, across the great lake are the triple snow peaks of Tongariro, Ngauruhoe and Ruapehu, with perhaps volcanic smoke or sulphurous steam curling up from the great crater scar on the upper slopes of Tongariro. From here, in about that same direct line, the curvature of the earth itself hides from view the Tongariro River Delta. To the left Motutaiko Island lies off the Hinemaiaia River mouth at Hatepe, and closer still, almost abreast of the Point lies the Waitahanui Rip, and beyond it still Tapuaeharuru Bay and the town of Taupo.

Away to the west on one's righthand side stand the great towering cliffs of Western Bays and on down the lake past the great bluff of Karangahape through Kuratau, Omori, Waihi, Tokaanu, to Turangi and the Tongariro where this lake encircling vision of splendour began.

Despite great snow-capped peaks and a sense of being encircled by mountains there is still a marvellous feeling of openness by the lake at Taupo. Somehow the sky itself seems bigger: almost as if that half-orb of the celestial sphere is more than one-half of the heavens. This I think is to do with optics. Lake Taupo lies 1177 feet above sea level. The air is not only thinner there, but as pure and unpolluted as any place on earth, beyond which the ever-changing clouds take on a magic unique to the place.

And that, approximately, is the setting. Immediately behind one on the Point itself lies this narrow littoral of rock, with virgin native bush overhanging it, and the call of bellbirds, tuis, fantails, even the fine summer song of the acclimatised English blackbirds and the chatter of chaffinches. A strange and enigmatic Maori rock carving stands sentinel in the little bay, tiki-like but phallic. Not far away, around the corner from Whakamoenga Point itself, in Okuta Bay, facing out to the distant Western Bays, is a sheer vertical rockface upon which are carved a fantastic phantasmagoria of real and mythological birds, beasts, and fishes.

The individual, widely separated carvings of strange beasts creep and sometimes even leap out of the natural rock, as if hiding behind them, or lie on natural ledges. The art and imagination, as well as the sheer size and splendour of the carvings are imposing, to say the least. Yet these are modern carvings, and such they remain, while the lone, wind- and weather-worn, lonely sculpture on the foreshore of Whakamoenga itself seems steeped with meaning and singularity of place and purpose. Old Maori burial caves lie almost hidden in the bush-clad slopes above the bay.

As far as is known in the oral Maori tradition there was never much of a permanent pa, or village, at Whakamoenga, but it was an important place on the route followed by the old canoes journeying from Waitahanui and Taupo to the distant settlements of Western Bays across the great lake. When the storm southerlies blow Whakamoenga Point is impassable from either direction. It becomes a dangerous lee shore, and is as much so today for powerful diesel engined boats as it was for the old Maori war canoes. In such adverse weather it became a safe haven, a port of refuge, until the storm blew itself out. At other times it was always a useful and safe place for an overnight stop on the voyages to and from Western Bays: hence its name 'A Place of Sleeping.'

In those ancient days there were no trout in the lake. In fact the lake waters were almost weirdly barren. There would have been teeming shoals of bullies, some isolated populations of the native grayling, now all but extinct. Not even the eel, so beloved of the Maori, because the Huka Falls always were, and remain, an impassable barrier to these creatures from the sea. Even the smelt were introduced to supplement the rich diet of koura, the freshwater crayfish, upon which the first trout grew to enormous size.

For me Whakamoenga meant trout, and trout I specifically fished for in order to catch and kill and eat, as opposed to the catch-and-release I practised by choice in the streams. Maybe it stemmed from this fundamental difference, for I no doubt fished with a different frame of mind as well as intention at Whakamoenga. It became a far from pot-fishing experience. In fact I probably fished more single-mindedly here, and with more intent – as well as probably better – than whenever I fished elsewhere.

There was also an incredible constancy in the quality of the fish caught at the Point. Other than for a month or so immediately following the winter spawning runs, when kelts often figured in the angler's catch (and these I always released), Whakamoenga rainbows were remarkably well-conditioned. They averaged around three pounds, with fish to six or eight pounds fairly regular for the consistent or purely fortunate angler, although I am quite certain that most of the superbly conditioned ten- and twelve-pounders sometimes hooked mostly made their safe escape by dint of the huge expanse of the lake, coupled with the often extreme difficulty of successfully netting a big trout from that steep and deeply indented shore.

The Taupo trout's diet of smelt, bullies and koura was indeed a rich one. There was a relatively flat shelf directly off the Point at Whakamoenga, about fifty feet deep, but not too heavily bouldered to snag too many of the angler's flies. Often enough, after being snagged, one would reel in a large freshwater mussel torn from the underwater rocks. But this flattish expanse was much favoured by the koura, the indigenous freshwater crayfish. The koura, likewise, was much favoured by the rainbow trout. One could always and immediately tell when one had caught a trout that had been dining well on koura – even before lifting it from the landing net – for the trout would rattle and crackle and crunch with the unmistakable sound of the koura carapaces rustling in the belly of the trout. Rainbows sustained on such a diet had orange-hued flesh superior to any salmon – and tasted better.

In eight years I never caught a brown trout there by day, although at certain times on fine summer days, from certain vantage points overlooking their specific territorial patrol routes, it was often possible to see big – really big – brown trout cruising by close by the rocks, within a few yards, but they seemed there and then uncatchable. Fishing for them was a frustrating and unsatisfactory experience. Better to cast well out beyond the cruising browns and go for the less educated rainbows.

Over the years I learned that the time to fish for big browns was at night, and best of all in that silent hour before dawn. At such times it needed quite a different approach. It was best to fish in the shallower bay directly in front of the lone Maori carving. I would sometimes be there at five o'clock in the morning, ready for the first legal cast of the day, and often the best time and the best cast for engaging a brown.

Long casting was not only unnecessary, but a waste of time and effort. Better to merely chuck out a few yards of fly line – preferably directly into the face of an onshore wind when the 'sea' and scend of the lake was foamed and troubled, piled up and breaking against the rocks. A small Red Setter or Hamill's Killer would sometimes need no more than a few retrieving tugs to engage a prowling nocturnal brown. Playing the hooked fish, and netting them out, was a different matter and often fraught with problems.

In boisterous weather – and at Whakamoenga there was plenty of it! – it was often difficult to get out a few yards of fly line into the teeth of a raging southerly. Moreover, in such conditions the 'seas' from the whipped up lake came crashing in over the rocks. It was not merely exceedingly wet, but sometimes exceedingly dangerous, and although elsewhere and in river fishing I generally reckoned to fish with a good measure of proper caution and regard for my safety, I must confess that here at Whakamoenga I sometimes fished foolishly and dangerously. Maybe I thought that because it was my own special place I understood its secrets and was safe there. Maybe I thought that eerie carved wind- and water-worn, phallic Maori spirit god immediately and close behind me was looking after my best interests.

Yet, in retrospect, looking back on some of those possibly foolhardy occasions I can only think that wild excitement drove me on. One early hour before the dawn the increasing southerly was still only whipping hard spray over the rocks. There were no 'seas' breaking over. I hooked and landed a good seven-pound brown trout within five minutes of arriving there, but hardly noticed that in the next fifteen or so minutes the wind increased to a good Force 7, and the build-up of the lake swell sent great waves crashing over the Point to my right.

I was drenched, but excited, and fished on. It was a struggle to lay out any line, but it was never successful to let the wind carry the line out: always best to cast across the wind when quite impossible to cast into it. With such 'seas' crashing everywhere I knew that even if I hooked a fish, it would be impossible to land it. It was dark and eerie, and I should have long ago retreated up the steep path and gone home, back to bed for a few hours as any sensible man would have done.

Perhaps I knew that I would hook another trout in that wild maelstrom of a lake, and wanted to see what it would be like. So – unwisely – I fished on. Sure enough I hooked another trout that tore around the little bay in front of the Maori statue in such a demented fashion, that, combined with the raging wind and crashing water, I had no real idea of in which or what direction the fish was running, or indeed whether it was running at all. I had a vague sense of disconnection from what was going on all around me. My fly rod and line seemed only wind-blown in my hand as I sought to re-connect with the trout, somewhere out there in the teeth of the gale and the stinging spray. A weird glow from the tripod Whakamoenga navigation light lit up the spume in its measured flashes. For a moment there seemed a lull in the wind. The trout turned out of the little bay – at least that's how I remember it – and started running, steadily, strongly, but unlike the histrionics of a rainbow, with the singlemindedness of a big brown. The lull in the wind was temporary or illusory and as it started to rage into my face the escaping fish did just that and kept on going – around the corner towards Rangatira Point. Then, with only the wind and raging water directing it, the fly line went slack.

I reeled in and went home. But I still had the seven-pounder and was not sufficiently chastised as perhaps I should have been.

But it wasn't always like that, fishing at Whakamoenga. There were days beyond reckoning when it was pure bliss just to be there, and to be fly-fishing as well, in sometimes bounteously yielding waters, was an added bonus.

Maybe it's because of the altitude – the surface waters of Lake Taupo are 357 metres, 1177 feet, above sea level – but New Zealand skies seem to have a remarkable clarity and quality rarely seen elsewhere in the world, and those above Taupo are especially so. On such days one can stand on the Point at Whakamoenga and feel a good long fly cast might reach half-way across the lake towards the snow-capped peaks of Tongariro National Park. Yet they are so far distant that, in England, they would be in the next county, or even the one after that. This clarity of the skies above is matched in the unbelievable clarity of the lake waters. What looks like three feet down is probably fifteen, and what looks like twenty feet deep is likely to be close to a hundred.

But the light itself is sharply deceptive. It is everchanging, almost minute by minute, so that with the passing of a cloud, or the shift of the sun across the arc of the sky, or even a sudden change in the breeze, can often in a flash reveal great cavernous previously unseen depths below, or, conversely, just as suddenly shut out all observable detail, as if the lake surface had become a leaden mirror. In high summer, with great shoals of bullies close inshore, and even great armadas of smelt hard up against the rocks, the trout come charging in at the forage fish. Sometimes the attack comes from a single cruising rainbow, but often as not the marauding trout come in numbers, herding the shoals of smelt from easy escape while the surrounding trout gorge themselves to satiety.

Many Taupo fly-fishermen relish the time of inshore smelting rainbows. Many Taupo artificial flies are streamers designed to imitate the smelt. There is no doubt it can provide exciting fishing but, like the evening rise, has as much myth about it as substance. To start with the smelt may be present in countless tens of thousands, and it seems a glorious optimism to suppose a cruising trout will select a single specific artificial when it's surrounded by dense shoals of the real thing – sparkling, twisting, translucent, exciting, full of the lifeforce compared with the sad tinsel and feather of the angler's artificial. Yet many do fall for the fisherman's lure – while tens of thousands don't. Over the years, fishing at Whakamoenga, I almost learned to steel myself against fishing for seen fish, or casting a fly into the melee of a trout attack on smelt. Instead, I generally stuck to fishing deep with a fast sinking line. Indeed, whenever I arrived there and the lake water around the Point was alive with smelting fish, or even greater numbers than usual of cruising, patrolling trout, I never rated very highly much chance of success. When it was possible to see rainbows by the dozen, and the surface waters were alive with their activities, I often came away fishless – and sometimes not a little frustrated. Deep down, fishing the lucky dip and grab bag of the invisible submarine world down there was the better strategy. Although I always hurried – even ran excitedly – to be casting a fly out into the expanses of the great lake, in all the years I fished there I rarely advanced straight out on to the Point from the bottom of the steep bush clad track that led down to the lakeshore. There was a deep-fissured indentation worn out of the volcanic ash rock, creating an inlet about four yards wide at its deepwater entrance, narrowing down to nothing over the twenty or so yards of its length. It was always a collecting place for the storm-tossed, water-smoothed lumps of floating pumice – such as once used to decorate the windows of old-fashioned chemist's shops, along with sponges, loofahs, and giant apothecary jars of bright red and blue and green liquids.

This narrow gut of water looked to be about three feet deep, but was ten or twelve. I always crept out from the bush track with the stealth of a hunter, with a few yards of fly line beyond the rod tip and the fly held ready in my fingers for instant despatch. There was often an inquisitive rainbow right up into the narrowing channel. One cast was all that was possible – again more of a chuck than a cast. It was either taken by the trout without any hesitation or rejected – upon which the alarmed trout would streak out to the safer, deeper, wider waters of the lake.

But the strategy of always being prepared for such a one-chance chuck paid off over the years with many good fish landed. If connection was made, it was instant, and with such a short line, and in such narrow confines, it was often possible to net the fish out almost immediately. Purists might balk at the notion, but with a prime four-pounder on the bank within a minute or two of arrival there, and before making a single proper cast, it was a good way to begin a few hours fishing, doing wonders for one's confidence.

There were enough places to fish on both sides of the Point to be quite alone. The few people who fished there with any regularity tended to stick to one or two choice spots, both of which yielded straight out into deep water. By clambering around and over a big overhanging rock it was possible to cross to a narrow outcrop overlooking Okuta Bay, close by the cliff-face of Maori situation sculptures, but quite hidden from it, and unapproachable by any than the one hidden path.

I sometimes went there by way of a change. It was just possible to get a decent backcast to clear the vertical side of the cliff in Okuta Bay, then to deliver the fly over and across a ledge of pellucid shallow water yielding beyond to dark depths always in shadow, no matter what time of day. A fly judiciously tweaked upwards through the deeper water just beyond the shelf would often bring a good trout chasing after it. But it was a cat and mouse game, far from conclusive at the outset. I never ever hooked a following fish either on the upward ascent of the fly, or after it came over the shallow ledge. If the trout

214

took it at all it was always in the single moment when the fly came over the extreme outer edge of the ledge. If it did so, it happened with an explosive bang and a jump clear of the water. If the trout spurned the fly in the split second beforehand, it would simply turn away and disappear into the depths. If it spurned the fly in the split second after it lifted into the limpid shallow water over the ledge it would dart like a demented creature along the length of the ledge, disappearing out of sight around the cliff face. Thus it happened on so many occasions that each encounter was played out like a re-run of the one before, resulting in a weird sense of deja vu almost every time I fished there. As it was exceedingly difficult to land a hooked fish, and there was only one tight and narrow spot where this was sometimes possible, the odds were on the trout's escape anyway. As I never did keep a fishing diary, I cannot be sure, but think it's probably fair to say that out of perhaps twenty or thirty good rainbows hooked in this tight little corner no more than half a dozen were ever netted and landed.

With few exceptions during the years I lived on the shores of Lake Taupo I rarely fished anywhere else but at Whakamoenga in the lake itself. It became a very special place for me, summer and winter throughout the year, by day and by night within the permitted fishing hours of 5 a.m. and 11 p.m., in fair weather and foul. I know enough about myself to realise it became a bolt-hole of sorts, as well as a place of solace and escape. Just as there should be, there were sufficient blank days to be good for my soul.

I never arrived at Whakamoenga without eager and high expectancy, and never came away from the place without a strange inner thankfulness that was something akin to worship. Most of my Taupo region fishing was done with one or two companions in the mountain streams of the central plateau away from the Taupo watershed itself. On those clear cold torrent streams I somehow felt a very much different sense of joy. These were mostly trout stalking waters; dry fly and nymph,

215

with all trout caught released unharmed.

Although the fishing was anything but easy, it all seemed so highly likely as well as probably that, as one's nymph would come tumbling down a riffle, or as one's dry fly came down around the bend of a stream into a pool, tucking into the bank under the overhanging flax or totoi, it was almost natural that it would be taken by an intercepting trout. It seemed a reasonable assumption that this would be the sequence and pattern of events.

Fly-fishing, however, at Whakamoenga into the vastness of a huge lake seemed to require sheer optimism bordering on imbecility. Although I have long been fascinated by other fishermen's reports of the sometimes almost paranormal aspects of fishing, and have never been one to dismiss them out of hand, I am not by any means a superstitious angler, in the way that many fishermen are. For reasons I cannot be pontifical about, I did, however, come to follow certain little rituals in going to, or coming away from, my fishing at this particular place.

It probably began with an early awareness of an acute sense of place when I went there. For reasons I only dimly understand, even in retrospect, I felt it was a great privilege just to be there, and to have all that magic fishing almost always entirely to myself was an even greater privilege. True, I did feel thankful to Bob Gower, a neighbour of mine in Acacia Bay along the road, who owned the Whakamoenga property and had given me his permission to go there whenever I wanted. To me this permission, and the key to the locked gate, was little short of the key to the kingdom of heaven.

But, that said and done, my thankfulness extended far beyond that which was due and proper to Bob Gower, the temporal owner of the place. Right from my first ever visit I was unshakingly conscious and aware of past occupiers and owners of the land, and felt at peace with their presence. The strange Maori carving at the bottom of the track at my favourite fishing place, standing erect gazing out across the great lake, soon became someone I spoke to. I was always very polite to him; greeting him by name on arrival, and asking his permission before beginning to fish. I always regarded the trout as his trout; yet the lake, and the entire country, was troutless in those earlier Maori days before Pakeha settlement. Even if I had to catch the trout – which I did with relish and, at least in that particular place, not a little skill – I still regarded the trout as a gift. And, because, despite becoming so familiar with every inch of the place, I was always a stranger, a visitor, an outsider, a foreigner, I always paid for my fish by throwing a coin into the water before the first cast.

There were not too many places around this little bay where it was possible to use a landing net with any ease and safety. It often varied according to the lake level, but generally speaking, my favourite place to do so lay directly in front of the Maori carving. I would mostly catch fish from the very snout of the Point (my good friend John Parsons always referred to it as the Bridge, and was convinced I favoured it in my loneliness there as a reminder of sorts of my days at sea, pacing the ship's bridge, as indeed was my habit), and having hooked and partly played a good trout from this promontory

I would walk it like a dog on a lead in and around the bay. Half way along it was necessary to negotiate a fissured inlet, when for a few seconds the trout had a good chance of making its escape. Once passed, and in front of the Maori carving, it was possible to slide down a rock, gaining a sometimes precarious foothold in a narrow pool, from which the landing net could be extended and the trout guided in, over the top. I would always heave, fish, net, and fly rod on to the flat escarpment three feet above, and almost directly in front of the Maori carving, and in so doing, I once realised, I was eye to eye with, and presenting my catch to Maui who, to me without much thought about it, was the god who inhabited that strange carved stone. And in a way I received the fish from him, not from the lake, and not by my own doing alone.

It was always a good place in which to think and let one's thoughts wander sideways, although I must confess, now in retrospect, that much of my thinking under the spell of Whakamoenga soon turned to fantasy. Why this should be I have no notion except to say that it always happened when I went there. Coming away from the place was like returning from a dream, and going back there was like resuming, re-entering that dream.

Now, writing this in England, half the world away from Whakamoenga, I am more than ever conscious of the strange affinity I had with this faraway place. Like most fishermen I sometimes fish vicariously in a world of dream and makebe-lieve. But nothing I've written about Whakamoenga is in any way to do with a fisherman's dreams or vicarious fishing. It was far more real to me than almost anything I've ever known.

And still is.

In the telling of this tale I have been particularly factual and prosaic, no more than hinting at some 'otherness' I found in this enchanted spot. In truth there was more 'otherness' than what passes for day to day reality at the bottom of that enchanted bush track to the rocks beneath, but I could not even begin to explain it, or even feel the need to try.

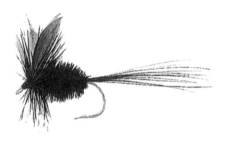

THE TIMARU STREAM
The Veiled River

Behold! human beings living in an underground cave, which has a mouth open towards the light and reaching all along the cave; here they have been from their childhood, and have their legs and necks chained so that they cannot move, and can only see before them, for the chains prevent them from turning their heads. Above and behind them a fire is blazing at a distance, and between the fire and the prisoners there is a raised way; and you will see, if you look, a low wall built along the way, like the screen which marionette players have in front of them, over which they show the puppets. And you see men passing along the wall carrying all sorts of vessels, and statues and figures of animals made of wood and stone and various materials, which are visible over the wall. Some of them are talking, others silent.

It is a strange scene that you describe, and strange prisoners.

They are like ourselves, I replied; and they see only their own shadows, or the shadows of one another, which the fire throws on the opposite wall of the cave.

True, he said; how could they see anything but the shadows if they were never allowed to move their heads?

And they only see the shadows of the objects which are being carried past. Suppose further that the prison had an echo which came from the other side, they would imagine when one of the passers by spoke that the voice which they heard came from the passing shadow. In fact, men in such a position would fancy that the shadows of the objects were the only reality.

And now look again, and see what will naturally follow if the prisoners are released and disabused of their error. At first, when any of them is liberated and compelled suddenly to stand up and turn his neck and walk and look towards the light, he will suffer sharp pains; the glare will distress him, and he will be unable to see the realities of which in his former state he had seen the shadows; and then conceive someone saying to him, that what he saw before was an illusion, but that now, when he is approaching nearer to reality and his eye is turned towards more real existence, he has a clearer vision, – what will be his reply? And you may further imagine that his instructor is pointing to the objects as they pass and requiring him to name them, – will he not be perplexed? Will he not fancy that the shadows which he previously saw are truer than the objects which are now shown to him? And if he is compelled to look straight at the light, will he not have a pain in his eyes which will make him turn away to the shadows which he can see, and which he will conceive to be in reality clearer than the things which are now being shown to him? And suppose once more, that he is reluctantly dragged up a steep and rugged ascent, and not released until he is forced into the presence of the sun itself, is he not likely to be hurt and annoyed? When he approaches the light his eyes will be dazzled, and he will not be able to see anything at all of what are now called realities. He will have to grow accustomed to the sight of the upper world. And first he will see the shadows best, next the reflections of men and other objects in water, and after that the objects themselves; then he will gaze upon the light of the moon and the stars; and he will see the sky and the stars by night better than he sees the sun or the light of the sun by day. Last of all he will be able to see the sun, and not mere reflections of it in the water, but he will see it in its own proper place; and he will contemplate it as it is. He will then proceed to argue that this is the power that gives the seasons and the years, and is the guardian of all that exists in the visible world, and in a sense the cause of all things which he and his fellows have been accustomed to see. And when he remembered his old home, and what passed for wisdom in the cave with his fellow-prisoners, do you not suppose that he would congratulate himself on the change, and pity them? And if they were in the habit of conferring honours and distinctions and rewards among themselves on those who were quickest to observe the passing shadows and to remark which preceded, and which came after, and which were together; and who were therefore best able to draw conclusions as to the future, do you think that he would care for such honours and glories, or envy the possessors of them? Would he not say with Homer,

> Better to be the poor servant of a poor master,
> and to endure anything, rather than think as they
> do and live after their manner?

Imagine once more, I said, such a person descending to the cave and taking his old seat there; would he not be certain, coming suddenly out of the sunlight, to have his eyes dazzled and blind?

And if there were a competition, and he had to compete in measuring the shadows with the prisoners who had never moved out of the den, while his sight was still weak, and before his eyes had become steady, would he not be ridiculous? Men would say of him that up he went and down he came without his eyes; and that it was better not even to think of ascending; and if any one tried to set free another and lead him up to the light, let them only catch the offender, and they would put him to death.

And now to apply my allegory. The prison– house is the world of sight, the light of the fire is the sun, and you will not misapprehend me if you interpret the journey upwards to be the ascent of the soul into the intellectual world according to my poor belief, which, at your desire, I have expressed – whether rightly or wrongly God knows. But, whether true or false, my opinion is that in the world of knowledge the Idea of Good appears last of all, and is seen only with an effort; and, when seen, is also inferred to be the universal author of all things beautiful and right, parent of light and of the lord of light in this visible world, and the immediate source of reason and truth in the intellectual; and that this is the power upon which he would act rationally either in public or private life must have his eye fixed.

Plato, *Republic*

One of the best of all the many and several fly-fishing delights for the peripatetic angler in New Zealand is that one sometimes comes across quite unexpected places that afterwards prove to have some magic about them that lingers on in one's memory, almost hauntingly. I wrote in another chapter of literally stumbling across a certain reach of the lower Kuratau River. For reasons I still do not prop-

222

erly understand, nor ever expect to, that particular experience was like stumbling into another world: a different world from the world outside it; as if curtains had been drawn aside for me to see into it, then enter into it. For all its charm and impact upon my senses it was still, however, rather like entering an alien world. It seemed to possess qualities of fantasy; yet it was not fantasy.

In sharp contrast the Timaru Stream of which I now write is very much a part of this world, of the world of everyday experience; yet by no means one likely to be experienced every day. Thus, in the manner in which I had once stumbled into the Kuratau River, so in this particular case I had journeyed to the Timaru Stream because it happened to be at the end of a minor public gravel road halfway along the eastern shore of Lake Hawea in the Southern Lakes of New Zealand. It had been my intention to seek permission to continue along the private road leading in to the Dingle Station, close by the famed Dingle Burn, beyond which lies a track leading to the Hunter River at the utmost head of the lake.

I have heard many people say that one of the things they least like about New Zealand is that there are so very many roads going nowhere; roads that simply worsen until at last they peter out altogether, and not necessarily at a farm gate, either, but simply peter out, there and then, coming to a dead end, as if whoever was building the road went away one day and never bothered to come back. Dead ends. Dead end roads. Wasted journeys. Wasted time. Always having to double back in order to get anywhere.

It was neither lightly, nor flippantly, that Samuel Butler chose *Erewhon* as the title of his novel about New Zealand as much as the 'nowhere' of its upside-down world of fiction.

For my part I have sometimes found that such dead-end, back country roads, instead of leading nowhere, lead to little paradises on earth. By not going down them, to the very end, one misses out on even the hopes of brief glimpses of paradise. Fortunately, such secret places are not on the tourist tracks.

Lake Hawea lies beyond the southeastern edge of the Mount Aspiring National Park, hard up against the Southern Alps. It has the great good fortune to lie close by the more tourist-popular

Lake Wanaka, so that itinerant travellers, hurrying to make mileage, generally come through the Haast Pass from the West Coast, skirt by the western shores of Lake Hawea, then carry on the short distance to the resort of Wanaka.

Hawea is a long, relatively narrow lake with a deep westward arm all but joining it to Lake Wanaka. The vivid blue of the lake betrays its enormous depth of more than four hundred metres, which extends for 65 metres below sea level. The lake has none of the beaches and gentle shoreline of neighbouring Lake Wanaka. These were drowned when in 1958 the lake was raised some 20 metres. Man's hand has intervened even here in manipulating nature. Water is stored in spring and early summer to be released in winter down the Hawea River and so to the Clutha River to feed the Roxburgh power station, when freezing temperatures in the Clutha's catchment area check its natural flow.

Despite its great depth and steep-sided shoreline there still exists one single island in the lake, Silver Island, close by the shore off Dingle Burn Station. One wonders whether it gave rise to the very domestic Maori legend concerning the mythological history of the lake – albeit that most Maori legends are at least in part historical.

In this tale two boys, Ono and Ruia, were flying their kites by the lakeshore, when the kites entangled and crashed into the water. For some reason insults were traded between the families of the two boys. Ono's father was wondering how he might rid himself forever of Ruia's family when a patupaiarehe – a spirit – came to him and taught him a song that, when sung, would detach a portion of land, sending it floating far out into the lake. Soon Ono's father was singing loudly, and soon the land where Ruia's family was sleeping had broken away and was floating out across the lake. A storm drove the 'island' aground – and it was transformed into a new land wilder yet more beautiful than any they had ever seen, and plentiful with berries, birds and fish. There Ruia's family built a new village and prospered as their descendants spread through the land. The floating island moved off again, to where it is not known. Perhaps it is floating still.

It well creates the backdrop to a floating world, in much the same way that the Chinese and Japanese have sometimes envisaged the world in which they live as similarly floating. The previously related fishing experience of fishing the Kuratau River, after stumbling upon it, is not entirely dissimilar from the following experience I was to have in climbing up the Timaru Stream that flows into this same Lake Hawea, not far in fact from Silver Island.

In those early days New Zealand was a troutless, salmonless land, and a happier intervention of man's dabbling with nature came a hundred years ago with the successful introduction of brown trout, rainbow trout, and quinnat salmon. The quinnat salmon here are landlocked but appear to survive in tenuous self-sustaining populations despite the unlikelihood of that happy coincidence seeming possible.

Man's intervention, already mentioned, of storing water in Lake Hawea in spring and early summer for release in winter, has proved to be beneficial to the trout. This is a particularly happy situation as all too often man's interventionist hand has a devastating effect on wildlife. When the lake level is low it tends to leave the extensive sloping banks a muddy quagmire. The fish change their feeding habits and are driven off into the depths. But as the trout population is governed by the food available, their numbers diminish during the low water periods that fortunately occur during the greater draw-offs in the winter months. With spring and the melting of the ice and increase of snow-water the lake level slowly rises. By the time the late spring rains augment the flow the lake water rises over the parched and mud-cracked steep margins. This is followed by a sudden and dramatic burst of insect hatching and larval activity – bringing the trout in in great numbers at the very time they most need this extra bounty of natural food. Nature has struck a happy balance. Fishing intensity is low, by any standards, even within New Zealand. It seems to ensure that the best and most successful fish survive and grow on, while avoiding an ever-increasing population of smaller trout competing for the same finite food supply.

But on the visit of which I now write I had no wish or intention to fish the lake itself. One of those inner urges – compelling but impossible to explain – directed me towards the Timaru Stream. It lay some twenty kilometres around the remote eastern lakeshore from the village of Hawea. I had anticipated there might be good fly-fishing in the lower reaches where the river entered the lake, but had not anticipated I would find undreamed of stretches, runs and pools up above, and almost totally hidden away from any fleeting, passing view.

The road to Timaru Creek follows the steep shoreline overlooking the lake. It is narrow and tortuous and towards its end descends a long and steep hill into the valley through which the river flows into the lake. Close by the lake, in a lovely tree-girt setting a captivating inlet divides stream and lake. It looked a most inviting place to fish – and so it was – but first I had this almost strange and compelling urge to explore upstream. The map indicated more river than seemed to be present, extending several kilometres upstream. Not far back from the lake the stream tumbled down through a steep and twisting gorge. Great boulders and rocky outcrops belied the more languid pastoral stretch towards the lake, only a few hundred yards away.

At first it seemed heavy going clambering up through the gorge, but then I moved out to one side to gain a better view of the terrain that lay ahead of me and found the faint traces of an easier-going track leading upstream, until I was climbing upstream along a ridge overlooking the fern and bush-clad narrow stream below. Nothing I was able to see looked at all fishable, except perhaps to poke a fly rod between bush to get

226

a fly on the water, but certainly nowhere where fly casting was possible.

After a climb through the gorge of about a mile – although it seemed longer – I came out into an almost flat valley floor, where the stream widened out into some small but splendid pools, with good runs and riffles between and a good flow of water that belied how little seemed to have been flowing through the secret-enclosing gorge. It was like stepping out into a new and different world. It was fishing perfection in miniature, yet the trout proved to be anything but, and were present (if not all catchable) in surprising numbers. The valley floor was wider and less rugged than the gorge, but still with sufficient upward gradient in the runs between the pools to maintain fast whitewater rapids favoured by rainbows. There was ample cover provided by manuka and matagourie scrub with the occasional twisted willow giving an even better upstream approach to the trout. I had expected to find clear water here, but was surprised at the gin-clear clarity. Even by looking in and under the faster white water at the necks of the pools it was still possible to see the sleek and silent waving of the dark tails of two rainbows pressed up hard where the stream bubbled through from above. More clearly seen were the lower orders of the rainbow trout echelons in hierarchic sequence – two, and a possible third I wasn't sure of – down towards the tail of the pool. If these plainly visible three- and four-pounders in full view were the junior fish present, I wondered at the size and weight of the pushy, dominant trout up front in the best feeding stations.

I went about it quietly at first, not knowing how much, or how little fishable water lay up ahead of me. Not wanting to spoil my chances in what might prove to be the best pool of all, I watched and waited, taking stock of the situation. As far as I could see there was little or no territorial patrolling by dominant trout, such as one might expect in most small rivers. Hierarchical distinction counted for less towards the tail of the pool, with the 'smaller' rainbows sometimes crossing and re-crossing each other's holding stations, with little or no apparent challenge or concern. Up ahead towards the white water, however, strict hierarchy ruled, and each and every trout knew its place in the scheme of things.

After watching and waiting for about fifteen minutes I could make out that occasionally a rainbow immediately downstream of the foam-flecked feeding lane would edge upwards in the water, apparently quickened in interest by some passing morsel about to float by overhead. Because of tricks of light in that dappled world, and the sunshine slanting along in the wrong direction, mirroring and leadening the fast water, it was hard to make out the sequence of events — except that I was sure I was seeing small dark mayflies coming off the water. As the odd one fluttered down the trout would suddenly drop downstream a yard or two, or even turn and dart downstream, then turn again in a flash and rise to intercept and take the fly before resuming station, exactly as before.

I tied on a small Royal Wulff dry fly; not in any specific attempt to match the fly on the water, but because a Royal Wulff floats high and rides fast water well, and I can not only see it all the way, but have great confidence in what it is doing out there. From where I stood I needed to cast over at least two smaller rainbows lying towards the tail of the pool. I wondered and feared that I might scare and scatter every fish in the pool, and leave them hidden away out of sight for an hour, but persisted with my folly of trying to get a dry fly to float down above the big ones in the front row.

Much to my surprise the lower echelon of trout were not lined and scattered by my first attempt, despite the clarity of the water. The dry fly alighted in the dark shadows at the very head of the pool, then came bobbing and sailing into view close by the outlying boulder past which the swirling water ran deep and fast and white. I saw the innermost rainbow twitch with sudden interest as the fly rode on by, but the line of float was at least a couple of yards away to the right.

Next cast I landed the fly right in midstream. Even before I saw it sailing out of the shadows I could see a trout I'd not even seen before rise up and engulf the fly on the turn, then streak downwards under the carpet of white water. It happened so quickly I had no time in which to mess it up at the strike. The line was fully extended upstream. I was not yet stripping in; simply holding the fly line in my fingers. No drag had taken its mad careering control. And the trout hooked itself in the process of taking the fly: something I can't recall ever happening to me before on a dry fly.

I knew at once it was a better than average rainbow, and also knew at once that in so small a pool, with a stony riffle above and a mountain of boulders at the bottom that the trout probably stood a better chance of escaping than I had of landing it. The taut and vibrating fly line cut through the water like a cheesecutter. I was able to scramble upstream almost abreast of the fish. Once I got it more or less under control – or so I must have thought – I could drop downstream again and net or beach the trout across the shallows on the other side.

From this new upstream position the light was kinder to my eyes. I could now see the trout clearly as it zigzagged to and fro across the head of the pool. Had it run straight up through the fast whitewater it might have gained its freedom in a few seconds, but it seemed obvious to me that the trout was so nonplussed about the whole matter it simply didn't know what to do next. Knowing enough about big rainbows to know it wouldn't be long in making up its mind, and that whatever it did would be dramatic and probably terminal, I threw discretion to the winds, waded out into the pool, then backed downstream, knowing full well that I was scattering and terrifying every trout it held.

My ruse worked. I held on as hard as I dared, but always using sidestrain, first to one side, then to the other. Then the tight line went sickeningly slack. As I stripped in line as fast as possible the rainbow somersaulted high into the air just a few yards in front of me. There were three or four great splashing jumps and a scattering of a myriad of bubbles every time. Just as I got back contact with the fish it bore away upstream again, hanging, driving into and under the fast water. I tried recovering some line by reel, but as soon as the trout felt that ratchety pressure it went berserk again and I could feel the fly line thrumming dangerously against underwater boulders.

As soon as I resumed hand-stripping in line combined with a low sidestrain the trout came after me. I waded back a few more paces, unhooked my folding landing net, flicked it open, and held it out in front of me, ready submerged, the handle stuck between my legs. Because it seemed to work, a combination of sidestrain, as much more stripping in as I dared, and more heave-ho than was probably wise, the trout was coming in towards me, only a few yards away. I held on, lifting the rod high now and grabbing the landing net handle, pushing it down in the water. The trout turned and was now heading downstream straight towards me, but straight into the net. I hoisted the net high, the handle buckling and twisting in my hand, but the trout was safely enmeshed inside and writhing like a tiger. Even as I watched I saw the Royal Wulff dry fly drop out from its hold in the trout's scissors, and wondered whether this was due to too much side to side change on my part in applying all that low elevation sidestrain, or whether the trout had been only lightly hooked all the while.

Then I slipped backwards, my foot sliding sideways into a trench between algae-covered rocks, into the stream and ended up sitting chest deep, but still clutching the enmeshed trout. It couldn't have been the prettiest of sights, and was far from being a picture of piscatorial elegance and skills. But I had that rainbow trout well and truly in the net. Had not one arm of the net collapsed and broken off the fish would certainly have made its escape, because it was now back in its proper element, immersed in water – as I was myself – for the net in which the trout lay imprisoned was wrapped around the fish like a winding sheet. I struggled ungainly to my feet, water oozing out from everywhere. By sheer good luck I still held my fly rod, the broken net, and the fish. I fell out on to the bank and started laughing. But I had my trout: a fine rainbow jack of just over five pound, which delighted my heart.

There was nothing for it but to leave that pool to recover from my intrusion, so I skipped the next upstream run, and the riffle above it that cascaded down from a small, tight pool above. There, I lightly hooked an acrobat of a rainbow of unknown but splashy size, so went on still further upstream to a long, fairly deep looking, rocky, ripply run that appeared to have a deep undercut bank on my side. Half a dozen offered dry flies trotted down alongside the steep bank were quite ignored. I changed over from the Royal Wulff to a yellow-bodied Humpy – always a favourite of mine when looking to claim the attention of apparently disinterested trout.

Cloud, and a westering sun were combining to make it hard to spot any trout from that distance below them, so I put on a weighted Hare's Ear nymph and tossed it up under the near-side bank. Nothing moved, apart from the artificial nymph tumbling back towards me. I was just about to change, or move on upstream, when the downstream tumble of my leader was halted, as if by a snag. I lifted, rather than struck, then the leader and fly line cut across to midstream and the trout took off up through the stony riffle.

Even while I was pleased that the running fish, stripping line off fast, was even playing to my advantage in heading straight upstream, despite the boulder-strewn water, I suddenly felt that awful slack and the tell-tale feel of an underwater bight of fly line being carried back downstream. Stripping in fast, I did make brief and solid contact once, but the trout turned yet again and came hurtling downstream at speed. I saw it writhe over the shallows where I stood, only a yard or two from my feet, and when the first weight came on the fish, it simply kept on going. The frayed and parted leader tippet had wedged between obliging boulders. When the weight came off it, the glistening nylon came back to me like a broken spring. There is nothing worse than to have a failed length of nylon monofilament suddenly remember all previous abuses as it corkscrews into useless curlicues.

After climbing out of the stream and finding a secluded place in which to sit in an open patch between the manukas I was assailed once more by that strange sense of daja vu as if this had all happened before, and was a re-run of some forgotten yesterday. I must confess it to have been an unnerving sensation: almost as if I had just woken up from a dream, only to find that the dream was actually happening, just as it had happened in the dream. There may be a perfectly logical and even simple explanation for this strange awareness, although I am at a complete loss to suggest one.

Although it has only happened to me on odd occasions, quite unexpectedly and without preamble or forewarning beginnings, and always while fly-fishing for the first time in certain special places, I cannot think it is in any way brought about by the act of going fishing – although I tend to believe this must be conducive to it: a sort of conduit of awareness. It may be something to do with fairly intense and single-minded concentration and the focussing of all one's senses upon a single objective in certain places and in certain lights. It might enter one's mind through the eyes by means of scintillating, dappled sunlight on running water – a sort of kaleidoscoping of the senses. At least those seem to be the necessary circumstances and conditions needed to bring it about. Yet I cannot think it has anything to do with fishing itself–albeit I often find an almost hypnotic haze flowing over me from the repeated, rhythmic, almost semi-automatic process of casting a fly again and again and again. However, I still have a sneaking feeling that it is a phenomena, and that it springs directly out of the place itself: certain places, that is.

To relate any more about these happenings has no place here, except perhaps to recognise and be aware of them.

It was time to go back across the valley floor, then clamber down through the gorge to the more immediate world of reality below, where the Timaru Stream meandered the short distance before debouching into the sunlit waters of Lake Hawea on its long journey back to the eternal sea.